APPLEJACK:

Pinkie Pie: Oh! ... it
the books. You s...

Twilight Sparkl...

Scootaloo: We are the Cutie Mark Crusaders!

Apple Bloom: And we want to crusade for our cutie marks!

Sweetie Belle: And, and, and we, um . . . Yeah, what they said!

Fluttershy: Rainbow Dash, you rock! Woo-hoo!

RAINBOW DASH: Look, ma, no wings.

Pinkie Pie: Cross my heart and hope to fly, stick a cupcake in my eye!

PRINCESS CELESTIA: I'm so proud of you, Twilight Sparkle, and I'm very impressed with your friends as well. It sounds like you're all learning so much from each other.

Photo Finish: Nervous? Don't be ridiculous. You're only facing a large crowd of ponies who will be watching your every move and silently judging you.

ZECORA: Maybe next time you will take a second look and not judge the cover of the book.

Discord: Make sense? Oh, what fun is there in making sense?

Rarity: Oh, woe is me! What ever shall I do? Ah! Dirt, dirt! Get away, dirt! Oh! Make it stop, make it stop! Ah! Filthy, disgusting dirt. It stings; it burns. Help! Oh, somepony save me. Save me!

PINKIE PIE: I, Pinkie Pie, declare that these treats are fit for a king, or a queen, or a princess!

Spike: Sometimes . . . when no one's around . . . I do this: *Lookin' good, Spike! Lookin' real good!*

SPIKE: You are a natural, Twilight . . . a natural disaster!

Once upon a time...

In the magical land of Equestria,

There were two regal sisters who ruled together
and created harmony for all the land.

To do this, the eldest used her Unicorn powers to raise the sun at dawn.

The younger brought out the moon to begin the night.

THUS, THE TWO SISTERS MAINTAINED BALANCE FOR THEIR KINGDOM
AND THEIR SUBJECTS, ALL THE DIFFERENT TYPES OF PONIES.

BUT AS TIME WENT ON, THE YOUNGER SISTER BECAME RESENTFUL. THE
PONIES RELISHED AND PLAYED IN THE DAY HER ELDER SISTER BROUGHT FORTH

BUT SHUNNED AND SLEPT THROUGH HER BEAUTIFUL NIGHT.

ONE FATEFUL DAY, THE YOUNGER UNICORN REFUSED TO
LOWER THE MOON TO MAKE WAY FOR THE DAWN.

THE ELDER SISTER TRIED TO REASON WITH HER,

BUT THE BITTERNESS IN THE YOUNG ONE'S HEART HAD TRANSFORMED
HER INTO A WICKED MARE OF DARKNESS, NIGHTMARE MOON.

SHE VOWED THAT SHE WOULD SHROUD THE LAND IN ETERNAL NIGHT.

RELUCTANTLY, THE ELDER SISTER HARNESSED THE MOST POWERFUL MAGIC KNOWN TO PONYDOM: THE ELEMENTS OF HARMONY!

USING THE MAGIC OF THE ELEMENTS OF HARMONY, SHE DEFEATED HER
YOUNGER SISTER AND BANISHED HER PERMANENTLY IN THE MOON.

THE ELDER SISTER TOOK ON RESPONSIBILITY FOR BOTH SUN AND MOON, AND
HARMONY HAS BEEN MAINTAINED IN EQUESTRIA FOR GENERATIONS SINCE.

The ELEMENTS of harmony

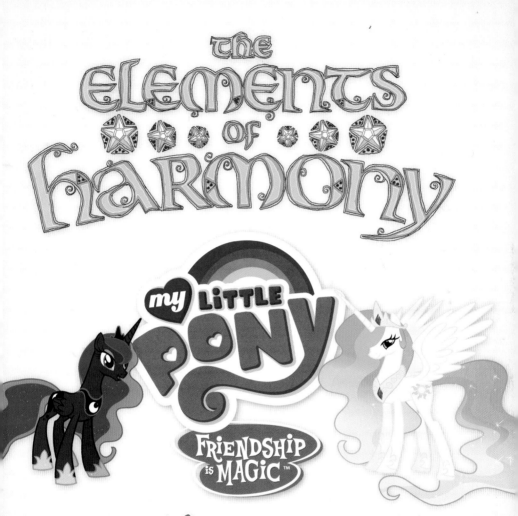

my LITTLE PONY
FRIENDSHIP is MAGIC™

THE OFFICIAL GUIDEBOOK

BRANDON T. SNIDER

LITTLE, BROWN AND COMPANY

New York Boston

Little, Brown and Company

Hachette Book Group
1290 Avenue of the Americas, New York, NY 10104
Visit our website at www.lb-kids.com

Little, Brown and Company is a division of Hachette Book Group, Inc.
The Little, Brown name and logo are trademarks of Hachette Book Group, Inc.

The publisher is not responsible for websites (or their content)
that are not owned by the publisher.

First Edition: June 2013

Book design by Charles Kreloff

Library of Congress Cataloging-in-Publication Data

Snider, Brandon T.
　My little pony : the elements of harmony : friendship is magic : the official guidebook / by Brandon T. Snider. — First edition.
　　pages cm.
　ISBN 978-0-316-24754-2
1. My little pony, friendship is magic (Television program)—Juvenile literature.　I. Title.
　PN1992.77.M87S65 2013
　791.45'72—dc23

2013000609

11

WOR

Printed in the United States of America

CONTENTS

A Few Words of Introduction... 12
by Jayson Thiessen and Meghan McCarthy

Why My Little Pony? 14
A foreword by Lauren Faust

1. My Little Ponies 17
Who's who among ponies in Equestria, featuring some early preproduction artwork

2. Cutie Mark Crusaders 37
Meet the youngest ponies and discover the special power of the cutie mark

3. Fellow Equestrians and Animal Friends 43
A roll call of other Equestrian residents of all shapes and sizes

4. The Dark Side 51
Meet some characters who aren't so friendly and read what the creators have to say about them

5. The Elements of Harmony 61
A history of the most powerful magic known in Ponyville

6. The Magical World of Equestria 67
A map of the land and details on the different regions

7. An Interview with Lauren Faust 76

8. Chronicles of Friendship 83
Summaries of each episode of the show, including friendship lessons

9. The Musical Pony 215
Complete song lyrics from the show, plus a few words from the show creators

10. Friendship Fanatics 249
An overview of the fandom, the appeal for fans of all ages, and a few words from the show creators

A Few Words of

Friendship.

It is something everyone needs in his or her life, but you have to make it happen—plant a seed, nurture it, grow it, maintain it, and keep it alive. Then, if we accept each other wholeheartedly and maintain harmony between us, that friendship is magic!

At least it is according to colorful, pretty ponies in a sparkly world of rainbows and cupcakes.

Somehow, the simple notion of these ponies making friends and being kind, loyal, honest, generous, and fun with one another sparked a huge following of people of all ages and genders around the world. But how did it happen? How did a children's cartoon geared toward little girls gain such a huge fandom?

This question has been answered many times in different ways, and if you ask me, friendship may be magic in Equestria, but in our world, *storytelling* is magic.

People love great stories, and I think that's the key to what makes this cartoon about little ponies so captivating to so many. Storytelling is about emotion: the feelings that the audience has toward the characters, the world, the situation, and the stakes.

This feeling doesn't come from the story itself; it's from *how* the story is told.

That's where I think *My Little Pony: Friendship is Magic* stands out. The combination of the writing, voices, design, storyboards, music and sound, animation, and timing—it's all designed to create a poignant feeling, one that you walk away with and stays with you all day.

A magical feeling.

Like friendship.

—Jayson Thiessen, supervising director

INTRODUCTION...

W hen Lauren Faust first approached me about writing for *My Little Pony: Friendship is Magic*, I had been on a bit of a creative hiatus. I had two small children and was still navigating the murky waters of motherhood. After ten years in the entertainment industry, I was trying to figure out which direction to steer my writing career, and, to be honest, I was struggling to find the right path. So when Lauren asked if I'd be interested in writing a few episodes, I jumped at the chance. I knew the show would be good, as I knew how dedicated Lauren was to the project and how important it was for her to create a show that featured strong female protagonists. But what I didn't realize was how much it was going to challenge me creatively and how satisfied I would be with the end result.

Ask any of the writers why they love working on *My Little Pony* and they will tell you how refreshing it is to tell stories that really mean something. We all feel like we are working on a project that isn't just entertaining but contributes something positive to the world. No matter your age or gender, it is important to be reminded every now and then that honesty, generosity, laughter, kindness, loyalty, and friendship are the keys to a happy and fulfilling life. *My Little Pony: Friendship is Magic* seeks to do just that—in a hilarious, music-filled, jaw-droppingly well-animated way.

I feel honored to work on the show and humbled by the support we've received from fans all over the world. If the show is half as fun for the viewers to watch as it is for us to make, then we are clearly doing something right.

—Meghan McCarthy, story editor

WHY MY LITTLE PONY?

A foreword by Lauren Faust

Rainbows, unicorns, fairy tales, hearts, stars, cupcakes, and, of course, pretty pastel ponies. Many people look at these things and roll their eyes. They can't imagine there could be anything more to such things beyond what they appear to be. But not little girls. They know something that we do not.

As adults, we observe that girls like these things. We absorb the information that this "frilly pink silliness" resonates with them, but we don't understand *why*. So when we interact with them, we try to give girls a slightly polished version of the so-called silliness our outsider eyes think they see. But when we present them with this inadequate interpretation, we sadly risk slowly convincing girls that our shallow representation is what they are actually imagining, and that the ideas in their heads are not as awesome and amazing as they actually are. If we are not careful, they will adopt our dismissive attitude that all this magic is merely "frilly pink silliness."

To truly understand, we adults must go inside ourselves and remember the time *before* the grown-ups told us these things were not worthwhile. That child is in there somewhere, and she believes unicorns are noble beasts that bring beauty to the world. She believes magical creatures are lovely and terrifying and the world they live in is one of wonder that has no bounds. She believes fairy dust is a powerful substance—what else in the world can so easily bring you your greatest desires? She believes the smallest, most helpless creatures can be your strongest support group if shown enough love. She believes something as simple as a cupcake can bring

...ogether in the bonds of friendship and a giggle is a welc...
...rm handshake.

...ot belittle this. To a little girl...This. Stuff. Is. *SERIOUS.*
...nagic is not frivolous and silly; it is huge, and it is glor...
...n her mind, it's something that not only garners wor...
...t also respect. She knows magic can give us everything...
...for, if only we give it the reverence it deserves.

...give little girls a respectful interpretation of the th...
...f we dare to take it as seriously as they do—we will se...
...hat it's not so silly at all. We can truly appreciate the ...
...it. And, amazingly, we can enjoy it ourselves.
...ild is in there, in each of us. And it's not so hard to find...
...en our minds to magic.

"Building a
universe is a whole lot of fun,
but sometimes very challenging. In
the early days of [the show] we would
often have big conceptual discussions . . . 'do
the ponies sleep in beds or stalls?' or 'if there
are no humans in this world, why would anyone
wear a saddle?' "
—Robert Fewkes, Hasbro Studios

"In her show bible, Lauren Faust really mapped out
the characteristics of the six main ponies. As we
wrote, characters developed, as they always do,
but their core characteristics were already
established by Lauren, giving us fantastic
groundwork to build upon."
—Amy Keating Rogers,
writer

My Little Ponies 1

TWILIGHT SPARKLE has a love of learning unmatched in Equestria. She is a natural leader, a patient friend, an obsessive organizer, and an avid reader. Her home in Ponyville is above the Golden Oak Library, where she also serves as librarian, assisted by Spike and her pet owl, Owlowiscious. Of the six Elements of Harmony, she represents the Element of Magic. As a young filly in Canterlot, she was

chosen by Princess Celestia to study the highest form of magic as the princess's apprentice. Seeing Twilight value knowledge over friends, the princess sent Twilight to Ponyville to learn the magical properties of friendship. Because Twilight not only mastered magic but also created magic of her own through such friendship, she has been bestowed with wings and the title **PRINCESS TWILIGHT**.

"In 'Lesson Zero,' Twilight has a meltdown over a looming deadline. My husband can attest to the fact that I have a lot of personal experience with this."
—Meghan McCarthy, story editor

Character concept art by Lauren Faust

Under orders from Princess Celestia, SPIKE THE DRAGON joined Twilight Sparkle in relocating from Canterlot to Ponyville. Twilight endearingly calls Spike her "number one assistant" for his extreme loyalty and ability to recognize when Twilight needs help. He has an incurable crush on Rarity, an insatiable appetite for sparkly gems, and the uniquely comical ability to messenger letters via his fiery dragon breath. Spike was found orphaned as an egg, and his origins remain a mystery.

"The fact that Spike sometimes feels like an outsider is a great place from which to mine stories. He's trying to figure out who he is. What beyond being Twilight's assistant is his role in this world? I think he really reflects how everybody feels at some point in their life."
—Meghan McCarthy, story editor

Ponyville library development art by Dave Dunnet and Martin Ansolabehere

19

Giggly, playful, and super girly, it's not unusual to find **PINKIE PIE** prancing and skipping blissfully through the streets of Ponyville. The silliest pony around, Pinkie Pie has a desire to entertain that makes her the most likely source for humor. She is a free spirit, often acting on her whims and following her heart. You would never guess she grew up on a dreary rock farm. Eager to amuse her friends and make everyone happy, Pinkie Pie will find any excuse to throw a party. She loves eating sweets and baking them so much that she is often found at the Sweet Shoppe in Sugarcube Corner, where she works, and lives in the apartment upstairs.

BLAH BLAH BLAH BLAH BLAH BLAH BLAH BLAH BLAH BLAH BLAH BLAH BLAH BLAH BLAH BLAH

Character concept art by Lauren Faust

"In 'The Last Roundup,' Pinkie had to annoy Applejack by blabbering on and on. I had come to that part of the scene and had no idea what Pinkie was going to say. But then as I was drifting off to sleep that night, I was thinking about the fact that Applejack and Pinkie were in a cherry orchard. Knowing Pinkie, she would be inspired by the cherries. Suddenly the words *chimi-cherry, cherry-changa*, and *chimi-cherry-changa* entered my brain. I jumped out of bed and quickly wrote those words down before I forgot. The next day, Pinkie was babbling about chimi-cherry-changas, pickle barrels, and kumquats and really getting on Applejack's nerves."
—Amy Keating Rogers, writer

RAINBOW DASH has one great all-consuming passion in life: to fly—FAST!!! Anypony who has ever seen this rainbow-haired Pegasus from Cloudsdale in the air has been in awe of her speed, agility, and confidence. Even in her youth, Rainbow was a fantastic flier, achieving what no other Pegasus had before: the Sonic Rainboom—a rainbow that shot out behind her like a jet stream! When any problem, big or small, arises, this aspiring Wonderbolt is the first to volunteer to save the day. Despite the mischief she causes, her friends are happy to have her around when danger is a-brewing, as Rainbow Dash proves time and time again that she is a true hero and a true friend.

Character concept art by Lauren Faust

"I personally enjoy working with Rainbow Dash as a character. She's fun, sassy, and excellent for using in action scenes!"
—Jim Miller, storyboard supervisor

RARITY could possibly be the most beautiful Unicorn you've ever seen, and she works hard to keep it that way—but she wants everypony to be beautiful, too! She uses her eye for detail, her creativity, and her Unicorn powers to find gems and make things sparkle! Her gorgeous designs are displayed at Ponyville's newest fashion salon, the Carousel Boutique. Rarity sees tremendous potential in her friends and always offers them makeovers or beautiful new clothes of her own design. Rarity's generous nature inspires her to make her friends as beautiful on the outside as she knows they are on the inside. Though she may seem entitled and prissy, Rarity has a heart as pure as gold.

Character concept art
by Lauren Faust

"It's really easy to label [Rarity] as emotional, superficial, and materialistic, but she's one of the more complex characters on the show....She'll pine for the attention of a prince, but drop everything to help out a friend in need."
—Brian Lenard, Hasbro Studios

APPLEJACK is Ponyville's resident farm gal! She lives just outside town at Sweet Apple Acres with her family. Applejack has come to be known as the most down-to-earth, resourceful, and dependable pony around. A talented arboriculturist, Applejack is the kind of pony who ain't afraid to get her hooves dirty. This hardworking Earth Pony is family-oriented and always ready to help Granny Smith or her little sister, Apple Bloom. Incredibly honest, Applejack would never stoop to telling a lie. However, her honesty and practicality keeps her from being as sensitive to others' feelings as she could be, despite her best intentions. Although Applejack can be a bit set in her ways, her friends know they can always count on this trustworthy pony to come through for them when they need her most.

"**M**y favorite [friendship] lesson is from [the episode] 'The Super Speedy Cider Squeezy 6000,' when Applejack writes to Celestia to tell her she didn't learn anything! Not exactly a 'true' lesson, but one of the funnier ones!"
—Jim Miller, storyboard supervisor

23

FLUTTERSHY is a natural beauty with gentle, serene ways. Despite her shy and unassuming nature, Fluttershy has a unique gift with animals. Her sweetness and sincerity can charm every animal, from tiny woodland creatures to the most powerful of mythical beasts, making her a valuable asset to her friends in all their adventures. Although she's afraid of heights (very embarrassing for a Pegasus) and shies away at the slightest sound, Fluttershy has no problem confronting grumpy manticores or scolding greedy dragons. While she lacks confidence, she has an inner strength that comes out when others are in trouble. Fluttershy has a lot of fears to overcome, but one day her strength of character and enormous heart will make her a force to be reckoned with.

"I think Fluttershy has shown a lot of growth. She is constantly struggling against her shy nature. And she's really making strides. She's confronted dragons, she's stood up to ponies who try to step all over her, and she's braved making a tornado. This is quite a lot for a pony who would rather just be having a picnic with woodland creatures."
—Amy Keating Rogers, writer

Character concept art by Lauren Faust

PRINCESS CELESTIA is the wise and kind ruler of Equestria. Governing her subjects from her castle in Canterlot, she emanates a commanding presence with both a Unicorn's horn and magnificent Pegasus wings. Princess Celestia is profoundly magical, and some say she is more than one thousand years old. With the help of her sister, Princess Luna, she makes sure the sun and moon rise and set each day.

Canterlot development art by Dave Dunnet and Martin Ansolabehere

Princess Celestia's younger sister, **PRINCESS LUNA**, has a history of difficulty living in her older sister's shadow. So difficult, in fact, her jealousy turned her into the villain Nightmare Moon! Fortunately, Luna was reformed and her heart softened by the ancient and powerful Elements of Harmony. Luna and Celestia have forgiven each other and are loving sisters once again, but Luna still has trouble adjusting to modern Equestrian life after her thousand-year-long banishment in the moon. Still speaking with ancient formality and finding it hard to move beyond her once fearsome image, she may struggle, but her intentions are pure and she is certain to find the happiness she seeks one day soon.

Development art by Lynne Naylor. Note that Luna's original name was Selena.

MY LITTLE PONY

PRINCESS SELENA

PRINCESS CADANCE is the ruler of the Crystal Empire. She is the former apprentice of Princess Celestia, who practically adopted her as a niece. Her love has a magical quality that combines with the magic of her husband, Shining Armor, to make them nearly unstoppable. She was the foal-sitter of a very young Twilight Sparkle, and the two remain great friends. They

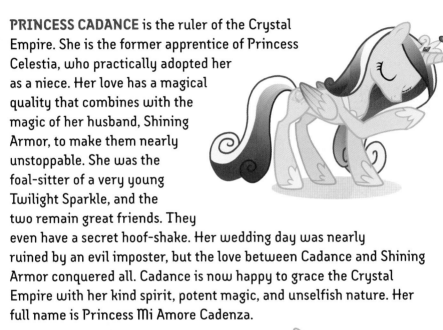

even have a secret hoof-shake. Her wedding day was nearly ruined by an evil imposter, but the love between Cadance and Shining Armor conquered all. Cadance is now happy to grace the Crystal Empire with her kind spirit, potent magic, and unselfish nature. Her full name is Princess Mi Amore Cadenza.

Featured in "A Canterlot Wedding, Parts 1 & 2," "The Crystal Empire, Parts 1 & 2," "Games Ponies Play."

SHINING ARMOR is the Unicorn captain of the Canterlot Royal Guard as well as the coleader of the Crystal Empire alongside his wife, Princess Cadance. He's also Twilight Sparkle's protective older brother, whom she affectionately calls her "BBBFF" (Big Brother Best Friend Forever).

Featured in "A Canterlot Wedding, Parts 1 & 2," "The Crystal Empire, Parts 1 & 2," "Magical Mystery Cure."

Ponyville Ponies

GRANNY SMITH is the wise matriarch of the Apple family and loves to tell a tale or two about the days of yore. Her memory may be fuzzy, but Granny's wit is as sharp as a tack. She was even one of the founders of Ponyville!

BIG MCINTOSH, also known as Big Mac, is the protective older brother of both Applejack and Apple Bloom. The soft-spoken colt generally doesn't have much to say, but he's always keeping an eye on his family.

If you're visiting Appleloosa, you're likely to be welcomed by **BRAEBURN**.

Featured in "Over a Barrel," "Apple Family Reunion."

The extended **APPLE FAMILY TREE** also includes Aunt and Uncle Orange, Apple Bumpkin, Apple Cider, Apple Cobbler, Apple Fritter, Apple Pie, Apple Strudel, Apple Tart, Buttercream, Caramel Apple, Golden Delicious, and many others!

Featured in "Apple Family Reunion."

See page 38 for Apple Bloom and page 39 for Babs Seed.

POUND CAKE

PADDY CAKE

THE CAKE FAMILY are the proud owners of Sugarcube Corner, Ponyville's most delicious bakery. The store is run by the kindly **MR. CARROT CAKE** and his wife, **MRS. CUP CAKE,** who make the tastiest sweets for every occasion. Pinkie Pie loves working in the bakery and often watches over the Cakes' twin foals, **POUND CAKE** and **PUMPKIN CAKE.**

As the mayor of Ponyville, **MAYOR MARE** is always prepared to do whatever it takes to help her people.

Featured in "Applebuck Season," "Winter Wrap Up," "The Mysterious Mare Do Well," "The Last Roundup," "Magic Duel."

CHEERILEE loves being a teacher at the Ponyville Schoolhouse.

Featured in "The Show Stoppers," "Call of the Cutie," "Hearts and Hooves Day," "Ponyville Confidential," "Family Appreciation Day."

29

FILTHY RICH and his wealthy family date back to the very founding of Ponyville. His daughter is Diamond Tiara.

Featured in "Family Appreciation Day."

ACE

DR. HOOVES

DAISY,
LILY VALLEY,
and **ROSE**

NURSE REDHEART
and DOCTOR

LOTUS
BLOSSOM

LYRA
HEARTSTRINGS

 SWEETIE
DROPS

BLOSSOMFORTH

SMARTY PANTS

GOLDEN
HARVEST

MINUETTE

MADAME LEFLOUR,
ROCKY, and
SIR LINTSALOT

BOWLER
PONIES

MARKET
SALESPONY

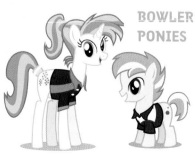

Canterlot Ponies

As Canterlot's resident fashion guru, **HOITY TOITY**'s been known to harshly critique the works of others, especially Rarity, who longs for his approval.

Featured in "Suited for Success," "Green Isn't Your Color," "Sweet and Elite."

PHOTO FINISH catches all the hot looks as Equestria's top fashion photographer. This trendsetter keeps an army of impressionable attendants with her at all times.

Featured in "Green Isn't Your Color," "Sweet and Elite."

SAPPHIRE SHORES is known for her music throughout Equestria as the Pony of Pop. The fashion-forward celebrity has a taste for Rarity's jeweled creations.

Featured in "A Dog and Pony Show," "Sweet and Elite."

FANCYPANTS is a high-society Unicorn who is fascinated with lower-class ponies, who he treats as novelties, though he claims no ill will toward them.

Featured in "Sweet and Elite," "A Canterlot Wedding, Part 2" "Too Many Pinkie Pies."

JET SET and his wife, **UPPER CRUST**, are Equestria's trendiest married couple. They have a taste for the extravagant and can be unapologetically snobbish about it.

Featured in "Sweet and Elite."

When a party needs the hottest music in Equestria, there's only one pony to call: **DJ PON-3**!

Featured in "Suited for Success," "A Canterlot Wedding, Part 2."

PRINCE BLUEBLOOD may be of a noble background, but he's also quite vain, which is no doubt why Rarity once had a crush on him.

Featured in "The Ticket Master," "The Best Night Ever," "Sweet and Elite."

OCTAVIA

Canterlot preproduction art

CloudSdale Ponies

THE WONDERBOLTS are an elite squad of Pegasus ponies who perform amazing aerial feats of derring-do at competitions across the lands of Equestria. **SPITFIRE** is team captain and a spirited competitor. **SOARIN** loves blazing a trail through the clouds—but only when he's not chowing down on one of Applejack's pies. Other team members include Blaze, Fire Streak, Fleetfoot, High Winds, Lightning Streak, Misty Fly, Rapidfire, Silver Lining, Surprise, and Wave Chill.

Featured in "Sonic Rainboom," "The Best Night Ever," "Wonderbolt Academy."

FLITTER, **STORMWALKER**, **THUNDERLANE**, and **LIGHTNING DUST**

Featured in "Hurricane Fluttershy."

MUSCLE PONY

BOY BULLIES

Cloudsdale preproduction art

"My cutie mark would
be a typewriter as, hopefully,
it is clear that my special talent
is writing. I'd go for a typewriter
instead of the laptop I really use to do
my writing since it is more fitting for the
not-quite-as-technologically-advanced
world of Equestria."
— Meghan McCarthy,
story editor

2

CUTIE MARK CRUSADERS

![My Little Pony logo]

> "Someone designed a cutie mark for me a while back. It's a piano keyboard with a large red musical note in front of it. I quite like it!"
> —Daniel Ingram, song composer

Apple Bloom, Scootaloo, and Sweetie Belle hoped that by trying a bunch of different things together, they'd get their cutie marks lickety-split! So the three friends formed a secret club called the Cutie Mark Crusaders, whose members were dedicated to trying as many things as possible. Although the fillies have tried many diverse activities, like baking and magic, their cutie marks have yet to reveal themselves. Unfortunately, some intolerant ponies have mocked the young trio for not being able to find their proper vocations yet. Thankfully, wise ponies such as Princess Celestia have encouraged the girls to not lose hope and to keep experiencing as many things as possible.

SWEETIE BELLE is a sweet-natured and sometimes spacey Cutie Mark Crusader with big dreams. Her quest for her cutie mark is not her only goal in life: Sweetie Belle longs for the praise and acceptance of her older sister, Rarity. Sweetie Belle has a blossoming talent for singing.

APPLE BLOOM is Applejack's little filly sister, and like her name suggests, she is full of potential but has a lot of growing to do. Although she is the leader of the Cutie Mark Crusaders, Apple Bloom truly has no idea what she is meant to do or who she is meant to be. As the "head crusader," she comes up with most of their (unsuccessful) cutie mark missions and spearheads their many (failed) efforts.

"My favorite story [in 'The Cutie Mark Chronicles'] is Pinkie Pie's. Playing against type is always fun, so having the most ebullient pony grow up on a dour, gray rock farm seemed like the right choice. It also provides a nice subtext to who Pinkie is. She has a soft spot in her heart for the ol' rock farm and loves her family, but at her core (or, at her cutie mark), she is totally different from this upbringing."
—Mitch Larson, writer

In addition to earning her cutie mark, SCOOTALOO is determined to learn how to fly. In fact, Scootaloo has fashioned herself a special pony scooter, and she uses her Pegasus wings not to fly but to propel her wheeled contraption through the streets of Ponyville! Scootaloo idolizes the adventurous Rainbow Dash and often tries to imitate her "too cool" attitude as well as her athletic skill.

BABS SEED is a tough-talkin' Apple cousin from Manehattan and the newest member of the Cutie Mark Crusaders.

Featured in "One Bad Apple," "Apple Family Reunion."

"We wanted to create a character who could bully the Crusaders but whose behavior was the result of an insecurity that the Crusaders could relate to and ultimately help her to overcome. We've got our three Crusaders in Ponyville and didn't want to add a permanent fourth, and we really liked the idea that Babs would come from out of town and be able to start up her own club with other ponies who hadn't yet gotten their cutie marks."
—Meghan McCarthy, story editor

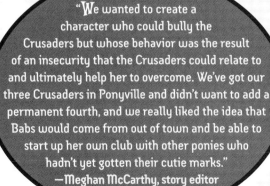

Other Young Ponies

DIAMOND TIARA and **SILVER SPOON** believe that money and expensive baubles can buy happiness. Together, the pretentious pair enjoy teasing young ponies who haven't gotten their cutie marks.

Featured in "Call of the Cutie," "The Show Stoppers," "The Cutie Pox," "Family Appreciation Day," "Ponyville Confidential," "One Bad Apple."

TWIST was picked on because of her blank flank until she discovered that her true talent was making sweet treats when two peppermint candy canes appeared on her hindquarters—her cutie mark!

Featured in "Call of the Cutie," "The Cutie Pox," "Hearts and Hooves Day."

SNIPS and **SNAILS** are two young Unicorns who are the best of friends. Snips is known for his enthusiasm, while Snails is known to be slightly more relaxed.

Featured in "Boast Busters," "The Show Stoppers," "Ponyville Confidential," The Mysterious Mare Do Well," "Magic Duel."

PIP SQUEAK, or "Pip" to his friends, is an Earth Pony from Trottingham, while **FEATHERWEIGHT** is a Pegasus pony as well as the editor in chief of the *Foal Free Press* newspaper.

Featured in "Luna Eclipsed," "Putting Your Hoof Down," "Ponyville Confidential."

Pony Power Makes a Mark

Growing up can be difficult, especially when it comes to finding your niche. Many young ponies in Equestria yearn to discover that special something that makes them unique and allows them to stand out in the crowd. Once they discover their true calling, a symbol known as a cutie mark magically appears on each ponies' hindquarters. Not all cutie marks are as literal as others, and many of them are simply meant to represent a positive feeling that the pony radiates to the world. But the road to finding one's true talent can be very frustrating for an anxious pony with a blank flank who's waiting patiently to bloom.

Before cutie marks appear, ponies must seek out life experiences so they can truly discover who they are and what their calling may be. It's important for them to try different things, put themselves in other ponies' hooves, and keep on learning as much as they can. There's no set age when cutie marks appear; they might come right away or years down the road. The key to unlocking a pony's true potential remains a mystery. But any elder pony will tell young ponies that even though the wait for a cutie mark may be difficult, it's more about the journey than the destination.

Scootaloo concept art by Lauren Faust

"It's not too hard to
describe what an animal
character might be feeling or
trying to communicate in a script;
the real challenge is up to the
storyboard artists and the animators
to make sure the emotions are
coming through in the expressions
and body language."
— Lauren Faust,
show creator

3

FELLOW EQUESTRIANS AND ANIMAL FRIENDS

ZECORA is a zebra who uses her ancient magic to cast healing spells from her enclave deep within the Everfree Forest. The ponies of Ponyville once believed her to be an enchantress who wielded the darkest of magic, but after admitting that they'd misjudged her, they befriended Zecora and often rely on her wisdom.

Featured in "Bridle Gossip," "Cutie Pox," "Luna Eclipsed," "Magic Duel."

"Zecora was supposed to be a second mentor to Twilight. I created her so that whenever the ponies had an adventure that needed a lot of explanation in the setup, they would have Zecora for a quick and simple source for exposition. (In fact, there was a scene where she did just that in the pilot, but it had to be cut for time.) Things just didn't pan out that way as we made the episodes."
— Lauren Faust, show creator

CHIEF THUNDERHOOVES is the wise and proud leader of the buffalo tribe that sought to reclaim Appleloosa from its pony settlers and repurpose it as a traditional stampeding ground. With the help of a young and agile buffalo named LITTLE STRONGHEART, the tribe was able to come to an agreement with the ponies, allowing them both to share the orchard.

Featured in "Over a Barrel."

CRANKY DOODLE DONKEY may be a crotchety old grouch who's reluctant to loosen up, but all that changed when the sweet-natured

MATILDA came around. Matilda met the cranky mule at the Grand Galloping Gala, where he began courting her as his "special friend." Matilda is the only one who's allowed to call him by the nickname "Doodle."

Featured in "A Friend in Deed."

IRON WILL is a muscle-bound minotaur who travels throughout Equestria as an inspirational speaker. He loves using his positive mantras and high-octane energy to get ponies up and moving. Iron Will has an enormous ego and often refers to himself in the third person because he loves to hear his own name.

Featured in "Putting Your Hoof Down."

GUSTAVE LE GRAND is a boastful griffon baker who believed his treasured éclairs would win first place at the National Dessert Competition. Gustave had some stiff competition from **MULIA MILD** and her famous "mousse moose," not to mention **DONUT JOE** and his mini city made of donuts known as "Donutopia."

Featured in "MMMystery on the Friendship Express."

Manticore development art by Lynne Naylor

MY LITTLE PONY   MANTICORE

A HAPPY

MAD OR SAD

MANNY ROAR, a manticore, is an intimidating sight with his lion's mane, scorpion's tail, and scaly wings, but this angry beast can be all bark and no bite, especially when he is shown a little bit of kindness.

Featured in "Friendship is Magic, Part 2."

STEVEN MAGNET, the sea serpent of the river, is quite a testy fellow. When Nightmare Moon cut off part of his mustache, he went into a tizzy. Thankfully, Rarity used her magic to solve the problem, and in return the sea serpent offered himself as a much-needed bridge to the other side.

Featured in "Friendship is Magic, Part 2."

DARING DO   **MS. HARSHWHINNY**   **CRYSTAL EMPIRE TOURIST**

Animal Friends

Fluttershy thinks **ANGEL** the bunny is just as cute as can be! But looks can be deceiving, because he's always keeping her on her toes with his bossy, demanding, and childish ways.

Featured in "Putting Your Hoof Down."

WINONA is Applejack's loyal work dog who absolutely adores helping her herd the flock.

Featured in "Just for Sidekicks," "The Last Roundup."

Be careful what you put in front of **GUMMY**, because he's likely to grab it! But don't blame Pinkie Pie's pet alligator so quickly. He doesn't mean any harm; it's just his nature.

Featured in "Just for Sidekicks," "Party of One."

OPALESCENCE, or Opal for short, may seem fluffy and sweet, but that's only when she's manipulating her owner, Rarity. This feisty little kitty has been known to hiss when she doesn't get her way!

Featured in "Just for Sidekicks," "Suited for Success."

"I do think Angel Bunny is one of the most conniving and willful characters on the show. He has Fluttershy completely under his cute little paw!"
—Jim Miller, storyboard supervisor

On the outside, PHILOMENA seemed like a poor, suffering, and squawking old bird, but Princess Celestia's pet had a secret. After losing her feathers and bursting into flames, she transformed herself into a beautiful phoenix.

Featured in "A Bird in the Hoof."

A **PHOENIX** is a mystical bird that sheds its feathers and is reborn in an explosion of brilliant flames.

Featured in "A Bird in the Hoof," "Dragon Quest."

OWLOWISCIOUS is Twilight Sparkle's adopted pet owl. At first, Twilight's assistant, Spike, thought he faced some stiff competition when Owlowiscious appeared, but he quickly realized that the bright-eyed bird was just being his regular helpful self.

Featured in "Just for Sidekicks," "Owl's Well That Ends Well."

Rainbow Dash assumed the little tortoise known as TANK was boring and slow, and could never be as exciting as she was—until he heroically saved her from a rock slide! Now she's proud to call him her pet!

Featured in "Just for Sidekicks," "May the Best Pet Win!"

PEEWEE became Spike's pet when he hatched from a phoenix egg! A group of bad dragons tried to persuade Spike to smash the egg when he found it, but thankfully he didn't. Now he and Peewee are the best of friends.

Featured in "Dragon Quest."

Character concept art by Lauren Faust

→ other rabbits, more normal

"I'm quite partial to Applejack's canine pal, Winona. She reminds me a lot of my own dog, Ripley, who just might be the best dog in the world!"
—Jim Miller, storyboard supervisor

"Gummy is my favorite. The idea of a toothless pet alligator is gold."
—Ridd Sorensen, art director

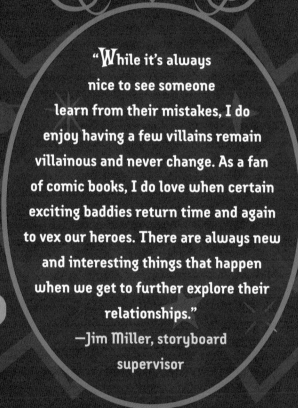

"While it's always
nice to see someone
learn from their mistakes, I do
enjoy having a few villains remain
villainous and never change. As a fan
of comic books, I do love when certain
exciting baddies return time and again
to vex our heroes. There are always new
and interesting things that happen
when we get to further explore their
relationships."
—Jim Miller, storyboard
supervisor

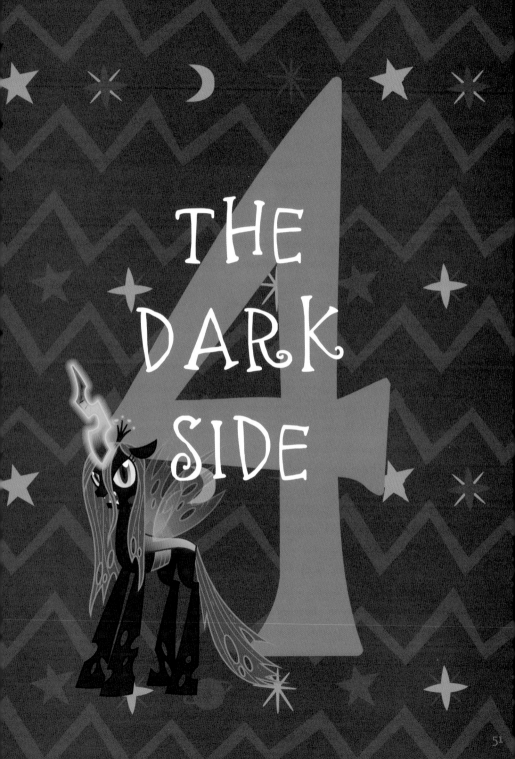

THE DARK SIDE

NIGHTMARE MOON is the maleficent alter ego of Princess Luna. In the dark form of Nightmare Moon, Luna is consumed with spite and enjoys manipulating unwilling ponies to do her bidding. Imprisoned in the moon, Nightmare Moon became even more dangerous when she escaped.

Featured in "Friendship is Magic, Parts 1 & 2."

Nightmare Moon concept art by Lynne Naylor

"I really enjoyed working with Rebecca Dart in creating Queen Chrysalis...though all I had to do was approve the amazing design!"
—Ridd Sorensen, art director

QUEEN CHRYSALIS is the shape-shifting leader of the changelings, a vicious group of creatures who are bent on destruction and mayhem. The queen even tried to take over Canterlot by using her powers to impersonate Princess Cadance and destroy the kingdom.

Featured in "A Canterlot Wedding, Parts 1 & 2."

CHANGELINGS are grotesque shape-shifting ponies who can morph their bodies into anything. These frightening creatures have fangs as well as insect features and translucent wings designed to scare even the bravest pony into submission.

Featured in "A Canterlot Wedding, Part 2."

KING SOMBRA ruled the Crystal Empire thousands of years ago but was banished and turned to shadow. Before he disappeared, the snarling black-hearted monster made the kingdom disappear and destroyed hope and love in the process. He recently returned but was thwarted by Twilight Sparkle and her pony friends.

Featured in "The Crystal Empire, Parts 1 & 2."

"The most underestimated villain on the show would easily have to be King Sombra. I think, if given the chance, he could do some serious damage throughout Equestria."
—Ishi Ruddell, animation director

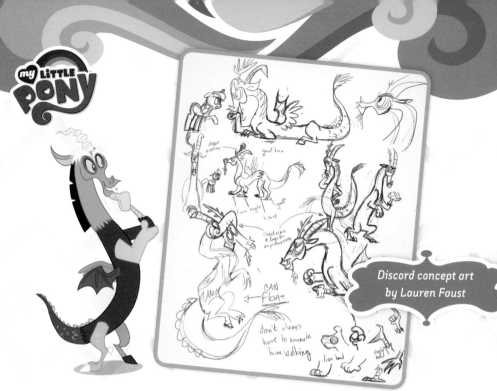

DISCORD is a draconequus, a rare beast with a pony head and a body comprised of many nasty creatures. He was once imprisoned in stone by Princess Celestia and Princess Luna but escaped, only to be defeated by the power of friendship. He's since reformed and struggles to keep out of trouble since he knows that Twilight Sparkle and her friends would use the Elements of Harmony against him if he ever unleashed chaos.

Featured in "The Return of Harmony, Parts 1 & 2," "Keep Calm and Flutter On."

"I don't think I'd want to reform all of our villains. I don't think that would be realistic. No matter how hard you try, some people (or evil alicorns) just aren't going to change their ways. But for a character like Discord, 'reforming' him allows us to tell new stories with his character. He gets to be the not-always-reliable ally instead of the known enemy."
—Meghan McCarthy, story editor

"Every character has room to grow and learn from their mistakes, and a good villain will still have a sense of humanity that can be related to. Otherwise they are just 'bad for bad's sake' and cannot be identified with. Not every villain we've had on the show has had a heart (that we've seen yet), but it's nice when we can work it in; it helps the viewer care about them...even when they're bad."
—Jayson Thiessen, supervising director

The traveling magician **TRIXIE** believes she's quite superior to other ponies and has been known to exaggerate her abilities from time to time. Recently, the Great and Powerful Trixie became remorseful once she was shown the error of her evil ways.

Featured in "Boast Busters," "Magic Duel."

GILDA is a mythical griffon, a creature with the head and wings of an eagle and the body of a lion! She was once friends with Rainbow Dash and loved good old-fashioned pranks. But Gilda's insecurities about being seen as cool caused her to fall out of favor with her friend.

Featured in "Griffon the Brush Off."

Gilda concept art by Lauren Faust

"I particularly enjoyed writing Flim and Flam. They are villains, but they are designed to be charming and disorienting. They speak very quickly. They finish each other's sentences. They're in constant motion. Everything they do is designed to dazzle and confuse people, so they can shake your hand while they're stealing your wallet. You can see their charm in action when the song ends and Apple Bloom is 100 percent ready to take their deal. This is the reaction the brothers are used to. In the midst of the song, one of the brothers confuses Applejack enough that she agrees to give them some apples for their demonstration. And when you're writing characters like that, their energy and optimism infuses the actual writing. I wrote that episode very quickly because their dialogue flew through my head as fast as it appears on-screen."
—Mitch Larsen, writer

The **FLIM FLAM BROTHERS** are a pair of salespony tricksters who travel from town to town, using song and dance to trick ponies into buying their wares. But it's all just a sham—the Unicorn duo are often run right *out* of town when their faulty products and shady tricks are revealed!

Featured in "The Super Speedy Cider Squeezy 6000."

The **DIAMOND DOGS**, known as FIDO, ROVER, and SPOT, may be big and brutish, but don't be fooled, because these canines aren't very bright. If you ever find yourself up against them, don't despair; their thirst for shiny gemstones makes them easily trickable.

Featured in "A Dog and Pony Show."

GARBLE is the teenage leader of a gang of fire-breathing dragons who challenged Spike to a series of trials to test his mettle. But these bad-natured bullies didn't take into account Spike's friends, who defended him using the power of friendship!

Featured in "Dragon Quest."

"Because we are writing for children, I think it is important for some villains to learn from their mistakes. Kids need to see that bullies and bad guys can change if given the chance. Sometimes kids may see these characteristics in other kids they know or even in themselves. If they then see that a villain can have a change of heart, then maybe they can implement that in their own lives."
—Amy Keating Rogers, writer

Other Beasts

Deep within the Everfree Forest live the dangerous **TIMBERWOLVES**! Few venture into the green so as not to come face-to-face with its dark protectors. It's been said that the howl of the timberwolf is the first sign of the yearly zap apple harvest.

Featured in "Family Appreciation Day," "Spike at Your Service."

The **COCKATRICE** is a rare beast that has the head of a chicken and the body of a snake. But don't stare at this creature for too long, because one glance from the cockatrice can turn a pony to stone!

Featured in "Stare Master."

Legend has it that **WINDIGOS** are cold winter spirits that are fueled by hatred and evil. The more hate that a Windigo absorbs, the colder the weather becomes. They're said to look like transparent, ghostly horses and can only be vanquished using the Fire of Friendship.

Featured in "Hearth's Warming Eve."

From the depths of the Froggy Bottom Bogg comes the **HYDRA**, a four-headed snake creature that guards the swamp from outsiders. Ponies always remember to step lightly because one false move and the hydra may devour them.

Featured in "Feeling Pinkie Keen."

PARASPRITES may seem sweet and innocent, but feeding these little insects may cause more trouble than they're worth. Their gluttonous appetites cause them to rapidly multiply, quickly turning them from pets to pests.

Featured in "Swarm of the Century."

Ancient myths say that CERBERUS is a giant three-headed dog charged with the task of guarding the gates to the nightmare realm known as Tartarus. This ferocious creature is responsible for preventing the evil trapped behind the gates from escaping.

Featured in "It's About Time."

Tucked away in the depths of the Ghastly Gorge is the QUARRAY EEL. The elongated creature gets quite agitated when anyone gets too close to a nest and has been known to try to eat any unwanted visitors.

Featured in "May the Best Pet Win!"

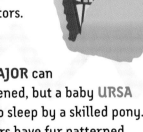

Momma bear URSA MAJOR can be big trouble if threatened, but a baby URSA MINOR can be lulled to sleep by a skilled pony. These two colossal bears have fur patterned after the glimmering night sky.

Featured in "Boast Busters."

Everfree Forest preproduction art

"I thought
it was important to
keep the Elements of Harmony
extremely revered. They began [on
the show] as a myth that no one believed
was true. They were hidden away in castle
ruins in a forbidden forest. When they're not in
use, they are kept in a vault in a stoic cathedral.
When they are used, they are used quickly and
powerfully, so they don't suffer the indignity
of just being jewelry to wear. Rather than
defining them, I felt it was important to
keep them mysterious, so it was left to
the viewers' imaginations just how
powerful they really were."
—Lauren Faust, show
creator

THE ELEMENTS OF HARMONY

he Elements of Harmony are six mystical jewels that harness the power of friendship. Little is known about the enigmatic Elements, but they're extremely powerful and can only be used in unison. Their mysterious origins are tied to Equestria's distant past, a time when two Unicorn sisters, Princess Celestia and Princess

Luna, used their magical powers to rule the lands. Celestia raised the sun in the morning, and Luna roused the moon in the evening. As time went on, Luna grew frustrated watching ponies play all day and sleep during the night. She felt her hard work was going unnoticed, and her seething anger and jealousy grew until they transformed the otherwise pleasant pony into the vengeful Nightmare Moon. Using her newfound abilities, Nightmare Moon plunged Equestria into darkness. Thankfully, Princess Celestia was able to harness the power of the Elements of Harmony to

stop her sister and exile her into the moon for all eternity. Balance had returned to Equestria, but Celestia knew that peace wouldn't last forever.

In the present, young Twilight Sparkle discovered a dark prophecy that heralded the return of Nightmare Moon on the longest day of the thousandth year. She desperately contacted Princess Celestia to warn her of the impending danger, but the princess dismissed Twilight's concern and insisted she focus her attention on the upcoming Summer Sun Celebration. Princess Celestia was convinced that the celebration would yield Twilight a number of new friends, and it certainly did. During the event, Twilight Sparkle instantly found five new pony pals: Fluttershy,

Pinkie Pie, Applejack, Rarity, and Rainbow Dash. It seemed, at first, that the prophecy was untrue, until suddenly Princess Celestia disappeared and Nightmare Moon once

again brought darkness to Equestria.

Twilight quickly realized that there was only one way to save the day. She and her new friends had to find and retrieve

the mythical Elements of Harmony from the ancient castle of the royal pony sisters! They traveled through the dangerous Everfree Forest and, after a perilous journey, finally arrived at the castle. During their quest, the new pony friends confronted a myriad of dangers that

brought them closer together in the process. Upon finding the Elements, the group was ambushed by Nightmare Moon, who seemingly destroyed the precious stones and doomed Equestria forever. But Twilight Sparkle realized that hope wasn't lost and that her new friends were the key to defeating Nightmare Moon. They each embodied the various aspects of the Elements of Harmony, and by working together, they pooled their power and used it against the vengeful Unicorn.

As Twilight called out the names of her friends, the broken

Elements re-formed into sparkling new pendants that gave each of their new owners a power of friendship! Applejack represented Honesty, Fluttershy embodied the spirit of Kindness, Pinkie Pie brought the group Laughter, Rarity exuded Generosity, and Rainbow Dash's strong suit was Loyalty. Twilight Sparkle embodied the Element of Magic, which only sparked when all the other Elements were present. Together, the ponies used their newfound powers to transform Nightmare Moon back into the

benevolent form of Princess Luna, once again bringing light to Equestria. With her kingdom now safe, Princess Celestia revealed that she knew Twilight Sparkle would be able to save the day by harnessing the power of the Elements. The princess then gave Twilight a special mission to chronicle the magic of friendship and report on the valuable lessons she learned. Over time, the Elements of Harmony have been used sparingly, in times of dire necessity, and never in a harmful

or hurtful way. When trouble arises, the duty falls to those six brave ponies to bring peace and order to Equestria once again.

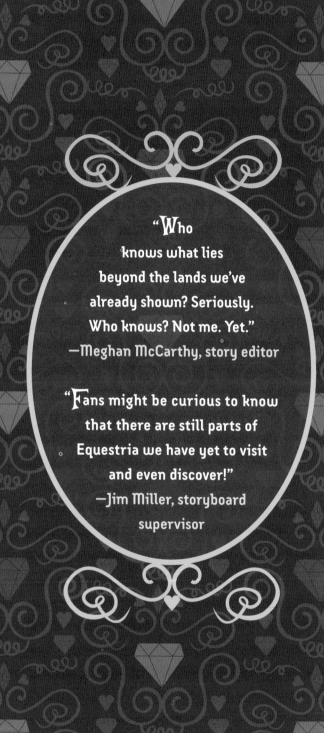

"Who knows what lies beyond the lands we've already shown? Seriously. Who knows? Not me. Yet."
—Meghan McCarthy, story editor

"Fans might be curious to know that there are still parts of Equestria we have yet to visit and even discover!"
—Jim Miller, storyboard supervisor

THE MAGICAL WORLD OF EQUESTRIA

EQUESTRIA

The enchanted lands of Equestria have become a beacon of hope and peace for everypony to look up to, but that wasn't always the case. The story of Equestria began in the distant past with three tribes of ponies, each with a unique skill: the horned Unicorns, the winged Pegasi, and the swift Earth Ponies. Every day, the Unicorns used their magical gifts to raise the sun in the morning and the moon in the evening. The Pegasi used their talents to create the weather, which helped the Earth Ponies use their skills to grow food. It seemed as if the three groups worked together, but the tribes lived separately from one another and rarely mingled. They were constantly arguing and demanding special treatment for the use of their skills.

All that changed on the day a blizzard caused a massive food shortage, and the three tribes were forced to come together to seek out a new home. They came upon a previously undiscovered land but began arguing over who had the right to claim it. Their negative energy began to grow and fueled the power of the evil creatures known as the Windigos! These ghostly beasts had caused the snowstorm in the first place, and they fed off the hatred and distrust among the pony tribes. Realizing that joining forces was their only solution, the three tribes were able to light the mystical Fire of Friendship, which cleared away the snow and defeated the Windigos once and for all. The three tribal leaders then decided to work together in their new home, which would henceforth be known as Equestria.

CANTERLOT

Canterlot is the noble capital of Equestria and sits high atop a mountain in the middle of the realm, overlooking the majestic, sprawling lands. The city is filled with beautiful golden spires, ivory towers, and sparkling waterfalls. It's also home to Princess Celestia and Princess Luna, who live there in the grand royal palace. Princess Celestia supervises Celestia's School for Gifted Unicorns, the place where young Twilight Sparkle learned to focus her powerful magic. Each year, Canterlot hosts the Grand Galloping Gala, and while the city may be filled with many high-society ponies, it serves to inspire the inhabitants of Equestria to come together in times of need.

PONYVILLE

Just down the mountainside from Canterlot is Ponyville, a small town founded by Earth Ponies and filled with hardworking, energetic ponies of all kinds. The sense of community is strong throughout town with businesses like Sugarcube Corner, a sweet shop run by the Cake family, and Sweet Apple Acres, a farm run by many generations of the Apple family.

Ponyville is also home to Twilight Sparkle and her bright-eyed friends, who keep themselves busy in the town's bustling marketplace. Whether they're reading a book at the Golden Oak Library or enjoying the annual Summer Sun Celebration, the citizens of Ponyville are a family through and through.

CLOUDSDALE

The whimsical Cloudsdale hovers high in the skies above Equestria and is populated exclusively by Pegasus ponies, who are the only ponies able to prance safely among the clouds. The billowing skytown is home to the speedster pony Rainbow Dash and also houses the weather factory, where the Pegasi make rainbows, snowflakes, and various other types of weather for the Earth Ponies below to enjoy. Each year, Cloudsdale plays host to the Best Young Flyer competition, which is held in the ceremonial Cloudeseum.

EVERFREE FOREST

On the outskirts of Ponyville lies the mysterious Everfree Forest, a wooded area filled with bizarre creatures, such as ursas, manticores, and timberwolves. It's

been said that the forest has an unnatural quality that puzzles the ponies of Ponyville. Animals are known to take care of themselves, plants grow freely, and the weather changes without the help of ponies. The forest once hosted the Elements of Harmony, which were kept in the ancient castle of the royal pony sisters. The mystical zebra Zecora lives deep within the green, where she practices her magic in secret.

THE CRYSTAL EMPIRE

The Crystal Empire is an ancient city that appeared on the frosty edge of Equestria after a thousand-year curse kept it secret. This historic area is set among an expansive mountain range and is inhabited by shimmering Crystal ponies. The Crystal Empire is rich with culture and led by Shining Armor and Princess Cadance, but it wasn't always.

A thousand years ago, King Sombra, a Unicorn whose heart was as black as night, took over the Crystal Empire. He was ultimately overthrown, turned to shadow, and banished to the ice of the arctic north. But not before he was able to put a curse upon the Empire—a curse that caused it to vanish into thin air. Even my knowledge of the Empire is limited. But what I do know is that it contains a powerful magic. If the Empire is filled with hope and love, those things are reflected across all of Equestria.

—Princess Celestia

WHITE TAIL WOODS

The lush greenery of the White Tail Woods is part of the annual Running of the Leaves, where ponies compete in challenges that include shaking the leaves off all the trees in the forest.

FROGGY BOTTOM BOGG

Froggy Bottom Bogg is a swampy marshland located south of Ponyville and is home to the multiheaded sea serpent known as the hydra.

APPLELOOSA

If you're looking for horse-drawn carriage rides and Wild West dances, then Appleloosa is the place for you! Saddle on up to the Salt Block saloon, because this little town on the edge of the Macintosh Hills has an old-time flavor. And if there's trouble in Appleloosa, a pony can always turn to the sheriff to help settle any disputes.

MANEHATTAN

Many young ponies dream of one day moving to the bright lights of Manehattan, a bustling island city on the northeastern edge of Equestria. With its large size and abundance of activity, Manehattan can be a lot for a pony to take in. Many

have made their home there over the years, including Applejack's high-society aunt and uncle, the Oranges, as well as the young Cutie Mark Crusader Babs Seed.

Cloudsdale (above) and Canterlot development art by Dave Dunnet and Martin Ansolabehere

This page, the ruins of the Castle of the Two Sisters in the Everfree Forest. At left, Fluttershy's cottage, the Sweet Shoppe and Ponyville. Development art by Dave Dunnet and Martin Ansolabehere.

AN EXCLUSIVE INTERVIEW WITH SHOW CREATOR
LAUREN FAUST

Are there any characters in particular that you enjoyed writing more than others?

I found myself getting excited when we would write episodes about Fluttershy. Fear and shyness seem like small things to overcome compared with some of the other ponies' more tangible challenges, but Fluttershy's challenges are very relatable. Experiencing fear is a very strong emotion, and, to me, the potential it brings is not just for great storytelling but [also for] great filmmaking. It is one thing to have a character *say* a feeling she's experiencing, but to make an audience feel it as well is more challenging. It needs to come across in all aspects of your story: acting, body language, staging, camera moves, timing, and music. Using those elements to get an audience to *experience*—not just understand—emotion is exciting to me, and I found Fluttershy was the character we could get that out of the most.

Aside from Twilight Sparkle, which character do you think has seen the most growth throughout the run of the show?

To me, that would be Pinkie Pie. She began just as a giggly, silly sort of girl with only a smidgen of a weird streak (breaking the fourth wall, appearing suddenly in unexpected places). There was concern, in the beginning, that Pinkie Pie would be off-putting because I made the mistake of pitching her as "hyper" and "ditzy." So we focused instead on toning her down and making her a simple "free spirit" in the first several episodes. But as everyone got more comfortable

Pinkie Pie concept art by Lauren Faust

with her, and as everyone saw how much humor we were getting from her, we were able to loosen the reins considerably. By the end of Season One, she was really over-the-top strange and bordering on crazy, with a wacky cartoonish magic all her own.

Were the characters' cutie mark origins already set in stone, or were you able to create them from scratch? Which one is your favorite? Why?

I had a couple of the ponies' origins worked out in the development stage. I knew Twilight went to school for magic and had some sort of immense power inside of her that, once it showed itself for the first time, would create her cutie mark. I also planned that filly Rainbow Dash was the only Pegasus in recent history to create a rainbow from speed alone, and that she only ever did it once. All the other ponies' cutie mark appearances were imagined in the writers' room when we were planning "The Cutie Mark Chronicles" [episode]. Rainbow Dash's story is still my favorite, just because it is so exciting and magical, and because of the way it touched all of her friends' lives.

A few of the villains have seen the error of their ways as the show has progressed. How important is it for these antagonists to grow and learn from their mistakes?

[Nightmare Moon's] reformation was integral to the plot of the pilot. For me, a lot of that story was extremely metaphorical. The Elements of Harmony were also the Elements of Friendship (a line that got cut), and I needed to think of something friendship would fix. I thought of the jealousy born of feeling ignored and left in someone's shadow. I thought that if we knew someone who was hurting that way, showing them friendship, showing them that they were loved and valued, would be the cure. Nightmare Moon was effectively blasted with a gigantic friendship cannon (as silly as that sounds!), and the love from that lifted her jealousy long enough for her to reconcile with her sister and regain her true form.

I think there's a double-edged sword to reforming villains. It's good to see them come around, because it shows us that people can change and that if you find yourself making a mistake, you yourself can change and be forgiven. However, I also feel it's actually important to show some villains remain villainous. Unfortunately, in this world, we run into people who will continue to hurt us no matter how much kindness we show them. It's realistic to show that this can happen and that it is best to cut abusive people out of our lives—like Rainbow Dash did with Gilda.

Which villain was the most fun for you to develop?
Discord was by far the villain who was the most fun to develop. By the time we were tasked with that episode, we felt some of the concerns over making the episodes too scary or confusing for our target audience were lifting. (For instance, Nightmare Moon was originally named Discord, but the name was rejected for fear children would not know what it meant.) I really held back on Nightmare Moon's frightening factor in the first two-parter, but it seemed less of a worry twenty-six episodes in, so we really went for it when it was time to make Discord.

When creating the visuals for these villain characters, were you looking to cast a balance between the light of the ponies and the darkness of their enemies?
I can't really say that was what our intention was. In fact, to address early concerns of frightening kids with villains and monsters, I tried to undercut the scariness by making Nightmare Moon beautiful, the manticore kind of cuddly, and the sea serpent silly. Early art of dragons depicted them as graceful and elegant. I always wanted there to be a sense of visual appeal to all the villains and monsters, avoiding anything gruesome or disturbing.

Who would you say is the most underestimated villain on the show and why?
I'd say Trixie. Jealousy is what transformed Luna into Nightmare Moon. I think Trixie's jealousy could have festered in her and made her a larger threat than she was. I think she has a huge amount of potential for becoming a significant villain.

Many of the creatures in My Little Pony are based on Greek mythology. What prompted that choice?
Incorporating Greek mythology into the show just seemed natural to me. Having Unicorns and Pegasi in the world of My Little Pony automatically opened the door to classic mythology—both European and Greek. Pegasi, in particular, are derived specifically from the Greek myth of Perseus's winged

horse, whose name was Pegasus. I wanted a recognizable, classic fantasy world, and Greek mythology is a well-known and abundant source for it.

Are there any characters that began as something quite different from what they ended up being on the show?
I originally intended for Twilight to struggle with the pressure she imposed on herself as Celestia's top student. I had hoped to show her biggest motivation for studying was to try to live up to what she believed Celestia expected of her and, as a result, Twilight had an occasional insecurity complex to deal with. I think the pressure to be perfect is very relatable to girls, and I thought seeing a character struggle with it and learn from it could be helpful and comforting. We touched on it a little in [the episode] "Lesson Zero." In the end, Celestia would know that Twilight's talents would come to light with patience and support, and Twilight would learn that trusting her instincts and going with the flow a bit more would make her a better student and better leader.

Luna was intended to have a lingering issue with Celestia. I wanted her to be a bigger part of Season One, but I worried about pushback for her "darkness" in the beginning. I meant for her to still need to learn how to feel good about herself in her sister's shadow, a lesson I thought could be valuable for girls with older siblings.

Who is your favorite animal pet on the show and why?
It's close between Opal and Angel. They both have so much personality. But I think Angel wins for being unexpected and funny.

Spike is unique in that he's one of the few nonpony main characters. How do you approach writing him and his struggles as opposed to the ponies?
I envisioned Spike as the sensitive little boy who has a lot of sisters and just seems to get along better with girls. I also imagined that he's much younger than the ponies and has a little bit of the vibe of a little brother who wants to

My Little Pony concept art by Lauren Faust

be included but can't really keep up. He's an outsider, and I think he feels it a little even though the ponies love and include him.

Each Element represents a positive quality a character should possess. What prompted you to choose these specific qualities?

It was quite a challenge, actually! When I was writing the pilot, I knew I had to come up with traits that defined friendship, but the trick was that these traits also had to be legitimately descriptive of the specific characters. Laughter and Kindness for Pinkie Pie and Fluttershy were obvious, but it took time for me to find an iconic friendly quality for Rainbow Dash, a character who I saw initially as self-absorbed and rather irresponsible. But Loyalty suited her well and brought out her positive traits. Rarity was the toughest. Originally, I chose Inspiration for her, since she's an artist, but others felt it was too much of a thinker, especially for kids. I'm so happy I found Generosity for her. It made me draw that aspect of her character out more in subsequent episodes, and I think that really helped pull her away from the stereotypical, unlikable debutante.

Are the Elements finite, or is there room for expansion?

I consider them finite. Three used to be wielded by Celestia, and three by Luna. I don't know what the new writers have in store for them. Though I had toyed with the idea of opposing Elements of Discord…

As we've seen, there aren't always musical numbers in each episode. What makes an episode song-worthy?

A song has to be integral to the plot. If it doesn't push the story forward, it's just fluff. For me, I always looked for instances where a lot of explaining needed to be done. Exposition, where characters are just talking about important information, can get extremely tedious. Getting the information across in a song adds a lot of extra entertainment value to something that would otherwise be boring to explain. I think "Winter Wrap Up" is a perfect example of this sort of song. I also think if there's something we want the audience to feel extremely excited about, a song is warranted as well. "The Grand Galloping Gala" in [the episode] "The Best Night Ever" seems so much more amazing in song than it ever would have been if the ponies were just discussing it.

"Winter Wrap Up" is still the most special song to me. It was our first big number and opened my eyes to all the potential of what music could bring to this show.

What's your process when creating a song? For example, does the script get written first, or the songs?
The script is written first. Many, but not all, of the writers will find a preexisting song that they feel has the tone or feeling they want to achieve and base the structure of their lyrics on that. Then the song goes to [composer] Daniel Ingram. I'm not sure if he utilizes the writers' reference for inspiration or not. He'll adjust the lyrics to fit his tune if he has to.

What is one thing that fans might not know about Equestria?
The ruins in the Everfree Forest where the Elements of Harmony were found were once Luna and Celestia's childhood home. It used to be part of Equestria, but the magical, uncontrollable forest encroached on it and they had to move their home to Canterlot. Perhaps the Everfree Forest is still creeping over the borders of Equestria…

February 2013

Dress designs for
"Suited for Success"
by Lauren Faust

"The challenge is delivering the message without getting too preachy or sappy. It's a tough balancing act and one we discussed a lot. We also didn't want the message to feel like it was shoehorned in. We wanted the message to feel organic and true to the story. I think we've been able to keep it entertaining because we bring humor to the situations so it won't feel too heavy-handed while still treating the message with respect."
—Amy Keating Rogers, writer

CHRONICLES OF FRIENDSHIP

The Magic of Friendship, Part 1

Welcome to the kingdom of Equestria—ruled by Princess Celestia, who maintains peace and harmony throughout the land. Twilight Sparkle, a young, scholarly student of Princess Celestia, is researching the legend of the Mare in the Moon, a tale of Princess Celestia's younger sister, who once tried to cast the shadow of night upon all of Equestria before being banished into the moon forever. However, Twilight Sparkle has discovered a troubling piece of information that claims Nightmare Moon will return to Equestria once again, on the longest day of the thousandth year, to bring about nighttime eternal. When she tries to warn the princess of this imminent danger, Celestia instead asks Twilight Sparkle and her pal Spike the Dragon to travel to Ponyville to check on the preparations for the Summer Sun Celebration. Twilight has been informed that her most important task is to simply make friends with the ponies of Ponyville!

It is only with Spike's urging that Twilight Sparkle tries to befriend the distinct ponies she comes across: Applejack and the enormous Apple family, Rainbow Dash, Fluttershy, Rarity, and Pinkie Pie. After strange experiences with each pony, Twilight wants nothing more than to get some time alone so she can continue her research on the mysterious six Elements of Harmony, the only way to defeat Nightmare Moon if she returns. But when she arrives back at her room, there is a surprise party waiting for her! Much to Twilight's dismay, the party lasts into the night until it comes time to watch the sunrise as part of the Summer Sun Celebration.

While everypony in Ponyville awaits Princess Celestia's arrival to raise the sun, Twilight Sparkle anxiously watches the moon. It appears exactly the way legend describes it will on the night of Nightmare Moon's return. The mayor announces Princess Celestia, and the curtain draws back to reveal…nopony! Princess Celestia is missing, and just as Twilight predicted, Nightmare Moon steps out onto the balcony with a sinister laugh: She has returned!

EPISODE 102

The Magic of Friendship, Part 2

Nightmare Moon has returned to Equestria, and Twilight knows she must find the Elements of Harmony. She prepares to head into the Everfree Forest to find the ancient Castle of the Two Sisters, when Rarity, Rainbow Dash, Pinkie Pie, Applejack, and Fluttershy assure her that they are coming along. As the ponies journey through the forest, Twilight begins to appreciate her new friends because they each have something to offer in order for them to get through their frightening quest. At last, the six ponies arrive at the ruins of the Castle of the Two Sisters, where the Elements of Harmony are embedded in five rock sculptures, each a different color gemstone. But the sixth Element is still missing, and Twilight must figure out how the five Elements together will spark the sixth. While the five ponies leave Twilight alone to concentrate, a strange purple smoke slithers into the room and creates a vortex, which sucks up the Elements. Twilight jumps in after them!

The ponies come back just in time to see Twilight face-to-face with Nightmare Moon, who is guarding the Elements of Harmony. Twilight attempts to create the spark to reveal the sixth Element, but nothing happens. Suddenly, Nightmare Moon shatters the Elements. It seems that the only way to defeat Nightmare Moon is destroyed! But with her new friends by her side, the solution dawns on Twilight Sparkle: The five Elements of Harmony—Honesty, Generosity, Laughter, Kindness, and Loyalty—lie within her friends! Together, the five Elements unite to spark the sixth Element: Magic! When the six Elements unify, Nightmare Moon vanishes as the magic from the Elements envelop her.

Princess Celestia arrives at the castle and reveals that she knew Twilight Sparkle just needed to let friendship into her heart. The ponies then see Princess Luna where Nightmare Moon once stood and learn that she is Princess Celestia's younger sister! The two sisters agree to rule Equestria together in harmony.

FRIENDSHIP LESSON:

I, Princess Celestia, hereby decree that the unicorn Twilight Sparkle shall take on a new mission for Equestria. She must continue to study the "magic of friendship." She must report to me her findings, from her new home in Ponyville!

EPISODE 103

The Ticket Master

While Twilight Sparkle is helping Applejack in the orchards, she receives two tickets to the Grand Galloping Gala to be held at Princess Celestia's royal castle in Canterlot. Twilight is about to ask Applejack to be her guest when Rainbow Dash appears and also wants to go! Suddenly, Pinkie Pie, Rarity, and Fluttershy are all clamoring at the chance to attend the Gala, and they each have a very good reason to go. Twilight Sparkle promises to decide which friend she will take.

Her friends quickly grow impatient waiting for a decision. Soon, all the ponies are doing favors for her, trying to improve their chances of getting the extra ticket: Rainbow Dash controls the weather in Twilight's favor, Rarity designs a Gala gown for her, Applejack bakes her all kinds of sweet apple treats, Fluttershy cleans Golden Oak Library, and Pinkie Pie throws her a party. After all this effort, Twilight decides she can't choose just one.

Twilight writes a letter to the princess, informing her that if all of her friends are not able to be there, then she won't be, either. Moments later, the princess responds with a ticket for each pony! The friends apologize to Twilight for putting so much pressure on her to make such a difficult decision.

FRIENDSHIP LESSON:

Dear Princess Celestia,
I've learned that one of the joys of friendship is sharing your blessings. But when there's not enough blessings to go around, having more than your friends can make you feel pretty awful.
      —Twilight Sparkle

Applebuck Season

I t's applebuck season at Sweet Apple Acres! Applejack is committed to picking every last apple on the farm while Big McIntosh rests his injured back. Just as she is about to begin shaking the trees, the ground rumbles, and an airborne Rainbow Dash warns Ponyville of a stampede coming its way! Everypony panics as the thundering herd of cows races toward the town. Applejack and her dog, Winona, catch up with the cows and manage to herd them away, saving the town center from disaster. The mayor is beyond grateful. She decides the town should throw Applejack a party, put on by Pinkie Pie!

With the party about to begin, Applejack is nowhere to be found. In fact, nopony has seen her in days! While they wait, Twilight Sparkle, Rainbow Dash, Fluttershy, and Pinkie Pie describe the ways in which Applejack is helping them with various jobs around Ponyville. Applejack sure sounds like a busy gal! The mayor announces that Applejack is the recipient of an award for her trustworthiness, reliability, and integrity. Applejack trots in to accept the award looking unusually haggard and even falls asleep on the stage. Twilight Sparkle knows something isn't right.

Applejack is overworking herself. Twilight tries to reason with her stubborn friend, but Applejack wants no help whatsoever—until another stampede hits Ponyville, this time caused by Applejack and Winona. Twilight is determined to get through to Applejack and returns to Sweet Apple Acres, where Applejack is barely able to stand up or stay awake. This time, Applejack can't say no to her friend's offer. Rainbow Dash, Twilight Sparkle, Fluttershy, Rarity, and Pinkie Pie all make time to help their friend finish the work in the orchards.

FRiENDSHiP LESSON:

Dear Princess Celestia,
My friend Applejack is the best friend a pony could ever have, and she's always there to help anypony. The only trouble is, when she needs help, she finds it hard to accept it. So while friendship is about giving of ourselves to friends, it's also about accepting what our friends have to offer.
Your faithful student,
Twilight Sparkle

EPISODE 105

Griffon the Brush Off

P
inkie Pie and Rainbow Dash are having fun playing harmless
pranks on their Ponyville friends, and it's brought them closer than
ever. So when Rainbow Dash's old friend Gilda the Griffon shows
up in Ponyville, Pinkie Pie can't help but feel a little left out. As the two
old friends bond over their days at Flight Camp, Pinkie feels increasingly
isolated. Gilda makes it very clear to Pinkie that Rainbow Dash is *her* best
friend and wants nothing to do with Pinkie Pie or her silly pranks.

Pinkie Pie takes her friendship woes to Twilight Sparkle and receives
some unexpected advice. Twilight suggests that Pinkie is jealous of Gilda

and it is Pinkie who needs to change her attitude. So Pinkie decides to look for the good side of Gilda, but this proves challenging when she witnesses Gilda pranking Granny Smith, stealing from the market, and scaring the wings off Fluttershy. Pinkie Pie knows what she must do and takes the matter into her own hooves: She throws Gilda a welcome party!

Gilda soon discovers that the party is rigged with harmless pranks meant for the guest of honor. Gilda's bad attitude rears its ugly head once more and everypony, including Rainbow Dash, catches a glimpse of the real griffon. When Gilda demands that Rainbow Dash leave the party with her, Rainbow defends her Ponyville friends. Rainbow Dash and Twilight Sparkle realize they've misjudged both Gilda and Pinkie. But Pinkie Pie has no hard feelings—just more pranks up her sleeves!

FRIENDSHIP LESSON:

Dearest Princess Celestia,
Today I learned that it's hard to accept when somepony you like wants to spend time with somepony who's not so nice. Though it's impossible to control who your friends hang out with, it is possible to control your own behavior. Just continue to be a good friend. In the end, the difference between a false friend and one who is true will surely come to light.

Your faithful student,
Twilight Sparkle

EPISODE 106

Boast Busters

When a new unicorn arrives in Ponyville claiming to have the most powerful magic in all of Equestria, Spike encourages Twilight to compete in a magic-off with this pony who calls herself the Great and Powerful Trixie. But Twilight doesn't want to be labeled as a show-off. Twilight endures Trixie's taunting and keeps her magical abilities to herself. Eager to see Trixie perform a powerful feat of magic, Snips and Snails retell the seemingly impossible story of how Trixie once vanquished a fearsome bear, the ursa major. The pair set off into the Everfree Forest to find an ursa major for Trixie to vanquish again.

Faced with a rampaging ursa, Trixie admits that she never vanquished an ursa major and has greatly exaggerated her powers. Twilight Sparkle puts her magical talents to use in order to protect Ponyville.

The townsponies burst into applause for Twilight as she worries that her friends will think she is showing off. Rarity, Applejack, and Rainbow Dash assure Twilight that they are proud to have such a talented Unicorn as their friend. Twilight reveals that the grumpy ursa they saw was actually a baby—an ursa *minor*. Embarrassed and with nothing left to brag about, Trixie gallops away from Ponyville.

FRIENDSHIP LESSON:

Dear Princess Celestia,
I have learned a very valuable lesson about friendship: I was so afraid of being thought of as a show-off that I was hiding a part of who I am. My friends helped me realize that it's okay to be proud of your talents, and there are times when it's appropriate to show them off... especially when you're standing up for your friends.
          —Twilight Sparkle

DragonShy

A slumbering dragon high up in the mountains is unaware that his snoring is releasing a cloud of smoke that threatens to cover Ponyville in darkness. To Fluttershy's dismay, Princess Celestia has bestowed the task of moving the dragon upon the six Ponyville friends. Rainbow Dash tries to persuade Twilight Sparkle to leave the terrified Fluttershy behind, but Twilight is insistent that their timid friend's talent for wild animals will be needed.

When the ponies arrive at the cave, Twilight assigns them each a task. It is up to Twilight and Fluttershy to enter the cave and wake the snoring dragon. But Fluttershy is too scared, so Twilight tries to wake the dragon on her own. He won't budge. Rarity, Pinkie Pie, and Applejack try to persuade the dragon to move, but their efforts backfire, and the dragon becomes very angry.

Seeing her friends hurt by the dragon makes Fluttershy angry and finally gives her the courage to confront the enormous beast. To everypony's surprise, the dragon starts to cry! Fluttershy (being the kind and understanding pony she is) politely asks the dragon to find a new place to nap where nopony's health will suffer from his smoky snores. Fluttershy's gentleness proves to be just as important as her friends' courage.

FRIENDSHIP LESSON:

Dear Princess Celestia,
I am happy to report that the dragon has departed our fair country and that it was my good friend Fluttershy who convinced him to go. This adventure has taught me to never lose faith in your friends. They can be an amazing source of strength and can help you overcome even your greatest fears.

Always your faithful student,
Twilight Sparkle

EPISODE 108

Look Before You Sleep

O n a rainy day in Ponyville, Applejack and Rarity are preparing
for a coming storm by tidying up loose tree branches around
Ponyville. Because they have very different styles of "cleaning,"
Applejack finds Rarity fussy, while Rarity thinks Applejack is crude. When
the storm bears down on them, Twilight offers them shelter in her home.
It's the perfect opportunity to try something Twilight has never done: a
slumber party!

While the storm rages on outside, Applejack and Rarity dread
spending another moment together but promise to keep their cool for

Twilight's benefit. Twilight consults her book *Slumber 101: All You've Ever Wanted to Know about Slumber Parties but Were Afraid to Ask* and plans sleepover activities for them, like makeovers and ghost stories. Applejack and Rarity can't play nice and begin bickering. Twilight demands they stop: Don't they realize they are ruining the only slumber party she has ever had? Just then, a bolt of lightning hits a tree outside, leaving a branch dangling dangerously over the neighbor's house!

Applejack springs into action, refusing to listen to Rarity's warning. After Applejack lassos the branch, it comes crashing into Twilight's bedroom. Realizing that she might need Rarity's assistance after all, Applejack apologizes to her friend for ignoring her warning. Even though Rairty knows it means her mane will get wet, she steps up to help Applejack with the branch, and the two are able to work together. Applejack and Rarity laugh at their differences and embrace what each has to offer.

FRIENDSHIP LESSON:

Dear Princess Celestia,
It's hard to believe that two ponies that seem to have so little in common could ever get along. But I found out that if you embrace each other's differences, you just might be surprised to discover a way to be friends after all.
          —Twilight Sparkle

Bridle Gossip

twilight is reluctant to believe the gossip being spread about the mysterious zebra named Zecora. While the ponies are speculating about how dangerous Zecora may be, Apple Bloom decides to prove how brave she is in the face of danger. She sneaks out and follows Zecora all the way to her home in the Everfree Forest. Upon noticing the young filly's absence, the six ponies dash out in search of Apple Bloom. They find her at the edge of the forest, hovering close to a strange blue plant. Zecora utters a mysterious warning toward the ponies, which the friends believe to be a curse. As the ponies head back to Ponyville, Twilight attempts to convince her friends that there is no such thing as a curse—but could she be wrong?

The following morning, the ponies wake up with strange ailments that they can only attribute to Zecora's curse. They retrace their steps to the Everfree Forest and brave their way into Zecora's peculiar hut. There, they witness her mixing ingredients in a cauldron while chanting. As the ponies surround her, Zecora tries to explain that the potion she is making is actually a cure for Poison Joke—the strange blue plant that is the real cause of their ailments. Twilight and her friends apologize to Zecora for judging her based on rumors and appearances.

FRIENDSHIP LESSON:

Dear Princess Celestia,
My friends and I all learned an important lesson this week: Never judge a book by its cover. Someone may look unusual, or funny, or scary. But you have to look past that and learn who they are inside. Real friends don't care what your "cover" is: It's the contents of a pony that count. And a good friend, like a good book, is something that will last forever.

Your faithful student,
Twilight Sparkle

Swarm of the Century

Fluttershy is gathering flowers near the Everfree Forest for Princess Celestia's arrival when she happens upon a cute little winged creature. Fluttershy brings the creature back to Ponyville to show her friends. But when she shows Twilight and Pinkie Pie, there are two more! Twilight offers to take one home and continues on her way to see how the rest of Ponyville is preparing for the princess's arrival. When she runs into Rainbow Dash and Rarity, they, too, are won over by the adorable creature—and two more have appeared! Rainbow and Rarity gladly take the other two. Pinkie says the creatures are called parasprites, and she's the only pony who doesn't want to take one. In fact, Pinkie is acting stranger than usual over the arrival of the parasprites.

The next morning, Twilight and Spike wake up to a room full of the fuzzy flying creatures, which seem to have multiplied during the night. They now have a swarm on their hooves! Something must be done before Princess Celestia's arrival, so Applejack herds the creatures back to the Everfree Forest. But when the ponies arrive at Fluttershy's cottage, the creatures are everywhere again. They infest Ponyville, eating all the apples and food.

To everypony's surprise, it is Pinkie Pie who solves the problem. Pinkie might look like a wacky one-pony marching band, but her music calms the parasprites as she leads the swarm out of Ponyville—just in time for Princess Celestia's arrival!

FRIENDSHIP LESSON:

Dear Princess Celestia,
I've learned that sometimes the solution to your problems can come from where you least expect it. It's a good idea to stop and listen to your friends' opinions and perspectives...even when they don't always seem to make sense.

—Twilight Sparkle

EPISODE 111

Winter Wrap Up

Winter is drawing to a close, and Ponyville's annual Winter Wrap-Up day is here. According to tradition, everypony in Ponyville is assigned a job to help prepare the town for spring—all of which are performed without magic. This is Twilight Sparkle's first Winter Wrap-Up. She is eager to find a way to help but wonders where she'll fit in.

It seems that every time Twilight tries to help a pony without using her magic, she isn't very good at the task. When she decides to use a little spell while helping Applejack clear snow from the farm, a mini avalanche ensues, setting the snowplows back an entire day's work. The mayor has become frantic about the state of Ponyville. Nothing is getting done and spring is going to be late—again!

The entire town is in chaos. Twilight, sensing the dire need for organization, visits each team to ensure a more organized fashion of work, until finally, flowers begin to bloom, bees buzz, and the sun shines! Twilight's involvement in bringing about spring proves effective, and she is even given an official title: the All-Team Organizer.

FRIENDSHIP LESSON:

Dear Princess Celestia,

Winter Wrap-Up was one of the most special things I've ever been a part of here in Ponyville. It helped me to learn that we all have hidden talents, and if we're patient and diligent, we're sure to find them. And as always, with good friendship and teamwork, ponies can accomplish anything.

—Twilight Sparkle

Call of the Cutie

Diamond Tiara is hosting a cute-ceañera party to celebrate getting her cutie mark. Apple Bloom is desperate to find a way to make her cutie mark appear to avoid further embarrassment. She tries everything from selling apples with Applejack to learning karate with Rainbow Dash to baking cupcakes with Pinkie Pie. When nothing works, Apple Bloom asks Twilight Sparkle to use her magic to make her mark appear—but even Twilight's magic can't help!

Confronted by the mean fillies at the party, Apple Bloom lies to Diamond Tiara and Silver Spoon about getting her cutie mark, but they call her bluff and begin to make fun of her. They are cut short when Scootaloo and Sweetie Belle speak up for Apple Bloom and blank flanks everywhere. They, too, are waiting for their cutie marks. Once Scootaloo and Sweetie Belle introduce themselves to Apple Bloom, they form an instant bond. They are ready to take on the world and discover who they are truly meant to be! The trio form a club and name themselves the Cutie Mark Crusaders.

FRIENDSHIP LESSON:

Dearest Princess Celestia,

I am happy to report that one of your youngest subjects has learned a valuable lesson about friendship. Sometimes, the thing you think will cause you to lose friends and feel left out can actually be the thing that helps you make your closest friends and realize how special you are.

—Twilight Sparkle

EPISODE 113

Fall Weather Friends

Applejack and Rainbow Dash are enjoying a competitive horseshoe game. When Applejack wins, Rainbow Dash is very disappointed—she *hates* losing. The two ponies play a series of games, but Applejack notices Rainbow Dash using her wings to get ahead. Applejack is furious and accuses her opponent of cheating. Rainbow Dash is somewhat insulted and challenges Applejack to race her in Ponyville's traditional race, the Running of the Leaves.

Before the race begins, Applejack makes sure that Rainbow Dash will not be able to use her wings to win the race by tying them up.

As the ponies line up for the start, they notice that Twilight Sparkle is running, too! Though Twilight admits this is her first race, she is confident that a slow, steady pace will take her to the finish.

After an ugly race, Rainbow Dash and Applejack make it to the end side by side, trotting over the finish line in a scuffle. It is a tie—for last place! Twilight Sparkle informs her friends that while her slow-and-steady pace did not get her first place, she was able to win fifth place! Rainbow Dash and Applejack sheepishly admit that their behavior during the race was less than respectful of their friendship.

FRIENDSHIP LESSON:

Dear Princess Celestia.
It's important to remember that the friendship is always more important than the competition.
          —Twilight Sparkle

8

Suited for Success

At the Carousel Boutique, Rarity is designing a beautiful gown to wear to the Grand Galloping Gala in Canterlot. Twilight Sparkle and Applejack enter, and Rarity decides that their Gala outfits are not suitable for a royal ball.

Rarity quickly produces five unique Gala dresses that fit her friends' personalities perfectly. However, when Twilight, Applejack, Rainbow Dash, Fluttershy, and Pinkie Pie see their gowns for the first time, they are not as enthusiastic. Rarity maintains her composure and begins changing the designs. The problem is her friends' picky requests are resulting in gowns that Rarity doesn't find tasteful. Just as Rarity finishes the revisions, Spike announces that Hoity Toity, a member of Canterlot's fashion elite, will soon be arriving in Ponyville to see a fashion show of all the Gala gowns.

Rarity is happy that her friends love their new gowns, but as the fashion show begins, she wants to hide—she knows the dresses are overdone and unattractive. Unfortunately, so does Hoity Toity. Upon seeing the gowns, the audience erupts in laughter. Her friends realize that they took advantage of Rarity's generosity. To make things right, they organize a private fashion show for Hoity Toity to see Rarity's original creations. Hoity Toity is impressed with Rarity's fashions and even offers to feature them at his exclusive boutique!

FRIENDSHIP LESSON:

Dear Princess Celestia,
This week my very talented friend Rarity learned that
if you try to please everypony, you oftentimes end
up pleasing nopony, especially yourself. And I learned
this: When somepony offers to do you a favor, like
making you a beautiful dress, you shouldn't be overly
critical of something generously given to you. In other
words, you shouldn't look a gift horse in the mouth.
                              —Twilight Sparkle

EPISODE 115

Feeling Pinkie Keen

I t's a normal day in Ponyville—until Pinkie Pie's tingling senses send a skeptical Twilight Sparkle into investigation mode. Twilight is reluctant to believe that Pinkie Pie's Pinkie Sense—twitches, shudders, and ear flops—can predict the future, even though it has made a believer out of some of her friends.

Pinkie is overcome by a dramatic shudder, the largest one she has ever experienced. And it means disaster—something big is going to happen at Froggy Bottom Bogg, where Fluttershy is headed! Applejack, Pinkie Pie, and Spike immediately set out to warn Fluttershy; Twilight tags along in an attempt to disprove Pinkie Sense. When the four arrive at Froggy Bottom, everything seems normal and Fluttershy is going about her froggy business. Twilight is about to have her "I told you so" moment when a giant four-headed hydra emerges from the water!

The friends escape, and they realize Pinkie Sense must have predicted the hydra. But Pinkie Pie is once again overcome by shudders, which means something big is about to happen again. Twilight admits that while she will never be able to understand Pinkie Sense, she does believe in it now. At last, Pinkie's shudders and twitches stop—making a believer out of Twilight was the big thing predicted by Pinkie Sense.

FRIENDSHiP LESSON:

Dear Princess Celestia,
I am happy to report that I now realize there are wonderful things in this world you just can't explain, but that doesn't necessarily make them any less true. It just means you have to choose to believe in them. And sometimes it takes a friend to show you the way.
　　　　　Always your faithful student,
　　　　　　Twilight Sparkle

EPISODE 116

Sonic Rainboom

Rainbow Dash is training for the Best Young Flyer competition, held in her hometown of Cloudsdale. She is determined to perfect a trick that has only been done once before—the Sonic Rainboom. As the day of the competition nears, Rainbow Dash grows increasingly nervous. Her friends want to attend the event in support of Rainbow Dash, but only Fluttershy, a Pegasus pony, can get to Cloudsdale. Rarity insists that Twilight find a way to use her magic to give them each wings, but Twilight manages to do this only for Rarity, who sprouts a pair of beautiful butterfly wings.

After Twilight casts a spell that allows Applejack, Pinkie Pie, and herself to walk on clouds, the ponies travel to Cloudsdale for the competition. Rarity's beautiful wings cause a stir in Cloudsdale, and Rarity decides that she, too, will enter the flying competition.

Rainbow Dash does everything she can to postpone her turn to compete, until finally only one chance remains. Now she will have to share her turn with Rarity, who took forever to primp herself. As the two friends perform, Rarity makes a big mistake and plummets toward the ground in the midst of Rainbow Dash's routine. Dash soars after Rarity to save her life, creating a Sonic Rainboom! Ashamed, Rarity apologizes for getting caught up in her own vanity instead of being there to support Rainbow Dash, who is awarded first place in the competition and a day with her heroes: the Wonderbolts!

FRIENDSHIP LESSON:

I learned how important it is to keep your hooves on the ground and be there for your friends.

—Rarity

EPISODE 117

Stare Master

he Cutie Mark Crusaders are planning for a serious cutie-mark-crusading sleepover at Sweetie Belle's. When Rarity has her hooves full at the shop and can't watch the three girls, Fluttershy steps up and offers to have the sleepover at her cottage. Rarity insists that the three young fillies are more trouble than they seem, but Fluttershy is confident she can keep them under control. Back at her cottage, Fluttershy has difficulty getting the fillies to calm down and go to bed, but eventually she persuades them to put off their crusading until the next day. After she tucks them into bed, Scootaloo, Sweetie Belle, and Apple Bloom notice from their window that a chicken has escaped from Fluttershy's coop—and is headed straight for the Everfree Forest!

The three friends manage to sneak out and follow the chicken tracks into the forest. Not long after, Fluttershy notices that the ponies have disappeared and follows the tracks, too. What Fluttershy stumbles upon is worse than she could have imagined. A stone statue of Twilight sits in the Everfree Forest, meaning only one thing: A cockatrice is on the loose! Fluttershy finds the fillies just as the cockatrice, a creature with a chicken head and the body of a snake, turns the escaped chicken into stone.

Fluttershy gives the cockatrice a healthy dose of her famous stare, demanding he turn Twilight and the chicken back from stone. Scared stiff by her look alone, the cockatrice obeys! The Cutie Mark Crusaders name Fluttershy the "Stare Master" and promise that next time, they will listen to whatever she says.

FRIENDSHIP LESSON:

I assumed that I'd be just as good with kids as I am with animals. Boy, was I wrong. I really learned the hard way not to bite off more than I could chew.
—Fluttershy

The Show Stoppers

Applejack has a surprise for the Cutie Mark Crusaders: a clubhouse! While it needs some work and renovations, the three young fillies are thrilled to have a place to practice their talents. The little ponies plan a series of adventures in an attempt to make their cutie marks appear but are sorely disappointed when their flanks are still blank. Scootaloo, Apple Bloom, and Sweetie Belle are close to giving up when Cheerilee informs them of the Ponyville school talent show. The girls set off to perfect a routine that is sure to get their cutie marks to appear.

The Cutie Mark Crusaders prepare for their performance back at the clubhouse, but they ignore Twilight's advice to stick to what they do best. Instead, the ponies take on tasks that they are unsuited for, masking their individual talents. When it comes time for the talent show, the three ponies perform their somewhat embarrassing routine and receive a round of roaring laughter from the audience. The girls are confused: Was it really *that* bad?

As Cheerilee announces the winners, the Crusaders hear their names called—for best comedy act! Though the ponies still don't have their cutie marks, they have discovered that maybe the way their marks will appear is by embracing their true talent—comedy!

FRIENDSHIP LESSON:

Well, maybe we were trying too hard...
—Sweetie Belle

...and instead of forcing ourselves to do something that's not meant for us...
—Scootaloo

...we each should be embracing our true talent.
—Apple Bloom

A Dog and Pony Show

Rarity is busy making a fabulous new dress dripping with diamonds when Sapphire Shores, the Pony of Pop, enters the Carousel Boutique. Sapphire falls in love with Rarity's bejeweled dress and wants three more, each covered in different gems! As excited as Rarity is to be dressing the pop pony sensation, she now must track down several jewels for Sapphire's dresses. While Spike and Rarity are collecting gems at Rambling Rock Ridge, three mysterious creatures are interested in Rarity's jewel-hunting skills. Just as Rarity and Spike are ready to head back to Ponyville, the Diamond Dogs make themselves known—and kidnap Rarity!

Spike runs for help. He and the rest of his pony pals go into an underground cavern. As Spike, Twilight, Applejack, Fluttershy, Pinkie Pie, and Rainbow Dash arrive at the end of a dark tunnel, they hear cries coming from behind a wooden door. They manage to get past the guards, only to find the Diamond Dogs with their paws over their ears, begging Rarity to leave.

The Dogs had forced Rarity to dig for jewels. Horrified at the thought of ruining her pony pedicure, Rarity complained nonstop to annoy her captors. Though Rarity prides herself on being a lady, she also knows how to get herself out of a sticky situation, gems and all!

FRIENDSHIP LESSON:

Just because somepony is ladylike doesn't make her weak. In fact, by using her wits, a seemingly defenseless pony can be the one who outsmarts and outshines them all.
　　　　—Twilight Sparkle

green Isn't your Color

At their weekly spa get-together, Rarity reveals to Fluttershy that Photo Finish, the famous fashion photographer, wants to have a photo shoot at the Carousel Boutique featuring some of Rarity's designs. And who better to model some of the creations than graceful Fluttershy? Though Fluttershy is reluctant, Rarity maintains that she is the best pony for the job.

Fluttershy's demure poses wow Photo Finish at the fashion shoot. Photo Finish wants to make Fluttershy famous across all of Equestria. Rarity is disappointed that her designs did not impress Photo Finish as much as Fluttershy's modeling, but she musters up a bit of encouragement for her friend. Fluttershy's modeling career takes off quickly. Rarity is soon jealous of the attention and fame her friend is getting and confides in Twilight.

Fluttershy then tells Twilight how much she hates modeling and that she is afraid to quit for fear of disappointing Rarity. Stuck in the middle, Twilight must make sure she does not reveal anypony's secrets. When Twilight's ploy to help end Fluttershy's modeling career fails, Rarity and Fluttershy recognize that hiding their true feelings is holding back their friendship. After reconciling their differences, Fluttershy is able to escape the chaos of the modeling world and Rarity finds confidence once more in her own fashion sense.

FRIENDSHIP LESSON:

Dear Princess Celestia,
Being a good friend means being able to keep a secret, but you should never be afraid to share your true feelings with a good friend.
—Twilight Sparkle

Over a Barrel

The ponies and Spike are all aboard the Friendship Express train to Appleloosa, where Applejack intends to plant the giant apple tree she has so tenderly named Bloomberg. Suddenly, a buffalo stampede nearly knocks the train off its tracks. The buffalo manage to unhinge and make off with the car carrying Bloomberg and Spike. In the confusion, Rainbow Dash and Pinkie Pie also go missing. Meanwhile, the others arrive at Appleloosa and are given a warm welcome from Applejack's cousin, Braeburn.

Rainbow Dash, Pinkie Pie, and Spike meet up in the desert and visit with the buffalo, learning about the herd that kidnapped Bloomberg. A young buffalo named Little Strongheart explains to the ponies and Spike how the Appleloosan settlers have planted apple trees on their traditional stampeding grounds, where their buffalo ancestors have run for many years. When Rainbow Dash, Pinkie Pie, and Spike bring their new buffalo friends to talk to the Appleloosans and the rest of the ponies, the Appleloosans refuse to move their orchards, and the buffalo insist they will stampede on their intended path.

The buffalo charge toward the settler ponies, and the settlers defend themselves by throwing pies. Then Chief Thunderhooves is hit in the head with a settler's apple pie and has a brilliant idea—the buffalo will allow the settlers to keep their orchard in exchange for some of their delicious fruit (and pie!). The Appleloosans compromise by making a stampeding path through their orchards. Peace is established between the two groups as well as the start of a new friendship built on understanding and sharing.

FRIENDSHIP LESSON:

Dear Princess Celestia,
Friendship is a wondrous and powerful thing. Even the worst of enemies can become friends. You need understanding and compromise. You've got to share. You've got to care.
—Twilight Sparkle

A Bird in the Hoof

Fluttershy is almost late to Princess Celestia's welcome brunch at Sugar Cube Corner, where she and her friends will finally be able to spend quality time with the princess. Twilight is incredibly nervous that her friends may not make a good impression on Celestia but is relieved when Fluttershy makes conversation with the princess about their shared love of animals. Princess Celestia points out her pet bird, Philomena, and Fluttershy is rather taken aback. Philomena is ragged and old, with a terrible hacking cough and an exhausted look about her.

Fluttershy sneaks off with Philomena and does everything she can possibly think of to revive the bird's well-being, from warm baths to aromatherapy. Despite Fluttershy's lifesaving attempts, Philomena seems to get worse and is losing more and more feathers!

When Twilight realizes that Fluttershy has kidnapped the royal pet, she's certain her friend will be banished, or imprisoned, or, worse, imprisoned in the place she's banished to. When the royal guards come looking for Philomena, the two friends panic. In the ensuing chaos, Philomena suddenly bursts into flames.

Princess Celestia arrives just as Fluttershy is sifting through the ashes that were once the bird. Horrified, Fluttershy awaits her punishment from the princess. But Celestia only laughs. Suddenly, a beautiful red-and-golden bird springs from the ashes. Philomena is a phoenix!

FRIENDSHIP LESSON:

I shouldn't have jumped to conclusions. Next time I'll ask before taking matters into my own hooves.

—Fluttershy

The Cutie Mark Chronicles

the Cutie Mark Crusaders set out to learn how other ponies earned their cutie marks.

Applejack tells of going to Manehattan in search of a new life. But the country pony wasn't cut out for the big city. Suddenly, a rainbow appeared over Ponyville, and Applejack knew her true home was back at Sweet Apple Acres. When she returned, her cutie mark of three apples appeared.

Fluttershy tells her tale of falling from a cloud and, not being able to fly, being saved by a flock of butterflies. Down on the land, she met all the critters and realized she could communicate with them. When a loud boom startled the critters, it was Fluttershy who was able to give them comfort. At that moment, her cutie mark of butterflies appeared.

Rarity's story is next. She was designing costumes for a school play and was unhappy with her results. With only hours until the play's opening, her Unicorn horn led her to a large gray rock. A loud boom suddenly cracked it open to reveal gems, which she then used to make her costumes spectacular. She realized she was destined to be a designer, and her diamonds cutie mark appeared.

Twilight Sparkle then tells about when her parents decided to enroll her in Princess Celestia's School for Gifted Unicorns. During the entrance exam, a loud boom triggered an unexpected magical surge in Twilight, which drew the attention of Princess Celestia, who took Twilight on as her personal student. Twilight earned her cutie mark and a special spot in Celestia's school.

Pinkie Pie tells the story of living on a rock farm, where everyone led a dull and gloomy life, until she saw a rainbow that inspired her to throw a party. Pinkie's party allowed her family to smile and have fun for the first time ever, earning Pinkie her cutie mark.

Rainbow Dash recounts the tale of racing to defend Fluttershy's honor. In the process, Rainbow Dash created a Sonic Rainboom. Fluttershy realizes that this event caused her friends to earn their cutie marks, meaning they all had a special connection through Rainbow Dash before they even knew one another.

FRIENDSHIP LESSON:

Dear Princess Celestia,

Today I learned something amazing! Everypony everywhere has a special magical connection with her friends, maybe even before she's met them. If you're feeling lonely and you're still searching for your true friends, just look up in the sky. Who knows? Maybe you and your future best friends are all looking at the same rainbow.

—Twilight Sparkle

Owl's Well That Ends Well

Spike is Twilight Sparkle's number one assistant. But when Twilight meets Owlowiscious while Spike is asleep, she makes him her junior assistant. Spike begins to suspect that Owlowiscious is trying to replace him. Every time Spike tries to help, Owlowiscious beats him to it, even providing his own feathers for Twilight's quill pen! When Twilight catches Spike in the act of trying to frame Owlowiscious for a terrible crime, she tells him he isn't acting like the Spike she knows and loves. Crushed, Spike runs away.

Spike finds a cave filled with gems in the Everfree Forest. Things are looking up, until the full-grown dragon who lives in the cave comes home. Just when things are looking really bad for Spike, Owlowiscious and Twilight come to the rescue. Owlowiscious distracts the dragon while Spike and Twilight make their escape.

Spike apologizes for being jealous, and Twilight apologizes for not recognizing how left out he was feeling.

FRIENDSHIP LESSON:

Dear Princess Celestia,

This is Spike, writing to you about my adventures. This week, I learned that being jealous and telling lies gets you nowhere in friendship. I also learned that there's plenty of love for every friend to share. So, from here on out, I promise that I, Spike, will... *ZZZZZZZ*

![My Little Pony logo]

EPISODE 125

Party of One

Everyone knows Pinkie Pie throws the best parties, and Gummy's birthday party is no exception. But when Pinkie invites her friends to Gummy's after-birthday party, she finds that they all seem to have other plans.

Pinkie begins to doubt her friends and, after secretly following them around Ponyville, decides they must not like her anymore. Saddened by this to the point that her hair straightens, Pinkie decides to have the party anyway—without her friends. But her new guests, a pile of rocks and a pail of turnips, aren't quite as much fun. Still, when Rainbow Dash arrives and invites her to come to Applejack's, Pinkie Pie refuses. Rainbow Dash doesn't take no for an answer and has to literally drag Pinkie Pie to Sweet Apple Acres. Once there, Pinkie Pie notices that her friends are having a party, which she assumes must be a "Farewell to Pinkie Pie" party.

Finally, it dawns on Pinkie that the party is actually for her birthday, which she somehow forgot about. Her friends weren't trying to avoid her; they were trying to surprise her!

FRIENDSHIP LESSON:

Dear Princess Celestia,

I am writing to you from the most delightful party. I'm not only having a great time with my friends but also was given the opportunity to learn a valuable lesson about friendship. Always expect the best from your friends and never assume the worst. Rest assured that a good friend always has your best interests at heart.

Your faithful student,
Twilight Sparkle

The Best Night Ever

t he ponies are attending the Grand Galloping Gala, the biggest event of the year in Canterlot. The ponies each have their own expectations of what is sure to be the "best night of the year": Twilight longs to spend quality time with Princess Celestia, Applejack is sure she'll have successful sales, Pinkie Pie just wants to party, Fluttershy can't wait to meet more woodland critters, Rarity hopes to meet her prince, and Rainbow Dash wants to impress the Wonderbolts. Spike, on the other hand, just hopes that the six friends will be able to spend some time together having fun.

At the Gala, each pony begins to realize that the night isn't quite living up to expectations: The princess is simply too busy greeting guests to speak to Twilight, the Canterlot ponies look down their noses at Applejack's homemade desserts, the woodland critters are terrified of Fluttershy, Rarity's prince turns out to be a pompous fool, and Rainbow Dash can't get a word in edgewise with the Wonderbolts. As for poor Pinkie Pie...well, her attempts to liven up the party are certainly not appreciated.

The six friends finally meet up again—in the midst of a disaster of their own creation. After fleeing the scene, they rendezvous with Spike at the local donut shop, where Spike says that he was right all along. If they had just hung out together, they would have had fun. Princess Celestia joins them and points out that the Gala is always terribly boring, but at least this year the six ponies made it interesting.

FRIENDSHIP LESSON:

Dear Princess Celestia,
Friends have a way of making even the worst of times into something pretty great.
—Twilight Sparkle

The Return of Harmony, Part 1

As Cheerilee guides the Cutie Mark Crusaders and their classmates through the Canterlot sculpture garden, she explains the symbolism of each statue. They reach a particularly grotesque statue representing Discord, "a lack of harmony between ponies." As they walk away from the statue, an ominous fissure appears in its side. Later in Ponyville, something is very wrong—the weather and wildlife are out of control. To Pinkie Pie's delight, it's raining chocolate milk! But the six pony friends and Spike agree the silliness is a real problem that must be solved. A letter from Princess Celestia arrives summoning them to Canterlot.

At the Canterlot castle, Princess Celestia reveals that her old foe, Discord, has returned and is responsible for plunging Ponyville into chaos. Celestia explains that the six pony friends are the only ones who can effectively wield the Elements of Harmony and vanquish Discord again, as she and Princess Luna once did. However, when the princess attempts to retrieve the Elements, they are missing! Discord appears, taunts the ponies, and leaves them with a riddle that will guide them to the Elements. The ponies head to the castle garden's labyrinth.

Once Discord has the ponies in the maze, he denies them the use of magic or flying. He continues with ploys to divide and conquer the friends by making them exhibit traits that are the *opposite* of the Elements they represent. Applejack becomes dishonest, Pinkie Pie hates laughter, Rarity becomes greedy, Fluttershy becomes cruel, and Rainbow Dash forgets her loyalty and abandons the cause. When Rainbow Dash flies away, Discord's "no wings or magic" rule is broken, and he declares the ponies have lost the game. It seems Discord has won. Will this be the end of the magic of friendship?

The Return of Harmony, Part 2

I t is Twilight Sparkle who realizes the Elements hadn't been in the labyrinth at all! She tries to lead the gang back to Ponyville, but her friends are acting more like enemies while under the spell of Discord's dark magic. It seems that something related to their dysfunctional new personalities is also turning their coats a dull shade of gray.

Twilight takes refuge in Golden Oak Library, where she enlists Spike's help to find a book about the Elements. Inside, she finds the Elements of Harmony themselves. However, none of her friends are happy to see the Elements. Seemingly devoid of hope, Twilight also turns gray. She tries to force the Elements onto their owners and unite them against Discord, but in their disharmonious state, the Elements have no power over him.

With Ponyville trapped in a state of chaos, Twilight heads back to the library, to find Spike waiting with heaps of mail from the princess. Twilight realizes they are all the letters she has written about friendship and understands, finally, that Discord has been trying to distract her from how powerful friendship truly is. The fate of Equestria rests on her friendships! She runs to each friend and snaps them all out of their trances. They successfully defeat Discord, learning that true friendship can overcome anything.

FRIENDSHIP LESSON:

We've learned that friendship isn't always easy. But there's no doubt it's worth fighting for.
    —Twilight Sparkle

EPISODE 203

Lesson Zero

I n a panicked frenzy, Twilight Sparkle realizes that she has not written Princess Celestia her weekly letter detailing a new lesson she has learned about friendship. She fears her oversight may get her sent all the way back to Magic Kindergarten, so she sets out to *find* a lesson about friendship. But she cannot seem to find anything worth writing about, and she is further disappointed when her friends don't seem to think her problem is worth worrying about.

Desperate not to disappoint the princess, Twilight decides that if she cannot find a friendship problem, she will have to create one. She enchants her beloved doll, Smarty Pants, so it will become irresistible to anypony who sees it. Her hope is that she can settle an argument among a group of young fillies when they fight over Smarty Pants, but of course, everything goes horribly wrong and soon everyone in Ponyville is fighting over the doll.

Amid the chaos, Princess Celestia appears and speaks sternly with Twilight. When all five of her friends butt in to stand up for her, they take responsibility for not being supportive of Twilight by not taking her stress seriously. With this, Princess Celestia decides that all six ponies should start reporting their findings about the magic of friendship when they discover something new.

FRIENDSHIP LESSON:

Dear Princess Celestia.
We're writin' to you because today we all learned a little somethin' about friendship.
—Applejack

We learned that you should take your friends' worries seriously.
—Fluttershy

Even if you don't think that she has anything to worry about.
—Rainbow Dash

And that you shouldn't let your worries turn a small problem...
—Rarity

...into an enormously huge entire-town-in-total-chaos princess-has-to-come-and-save-the-day problem!
—Pinkie Pie

Signed, your loyal subjects.
—Applejack

EPISODE 204

Luna Eclipsed

t is Nightmare Night in Ponyville (the Equestrian equivalent of
Halloween). Twilight Sparkle wanders the festival dressed as Star
Swirl the Bearded, meeting her friends and checking out all the
costumes. Zecora recites the tale of Nightmare Moon, describing the
annual festival where everypony must dress up in elaborate costumes
so that when Nightmare Moon flies over Equestria, she sees no ponies
to gobble up and leaves them alone.

In the midst of all this, Princess Luna (formerly Nightmare Moon)
arrives, scaring all the ponies. Luna tries to show Ponyville there is
no need to fear her, but after spending a thousand years trapped in
the moon, her social skills are a bit rusty. Twilight isn't scared and
enlists the help of her best friends to give Luna tips on how to become

approachable. Step one: Lose the roaring, antiquated royal Canterlot voice. Luna succeeds at first, though her patience wears thin and she slips back into her old ways, causing Ponyville to scatter in fear once again. Angered that she is not loved by her subjects, Luna vows to cancel the Nightmare Night celebration forever.

Pinkie Pie is not helping Twilight's mission, spreading panic among the already-scared residents of Ponyville. When Twilight confronts Pinkie about her insensitive behavior, Pinkie reveals she was doing it on purpose because sometimes, it's simply *fun* to be scared—it is the point of the whole festival, after all. Twilight gets an idea and instructs the princess to play along as Nightmare Moon for the night. When Luna sees how much the ponies really do enjoy the festival and how much they love her playing the character, she agrees to reinstate Nightmare Night. Twilight learns that friendship is best when the gift is shared and you help others learn how to find and use it as well, just as she did with Princess Luna.

FRIENDSHIP LESSON:

Dear Princess Celestia,
When you first sent me to Ponyville, I didn't know anything about friendship. I met somepony tonight who was having the same problem—your sister, Princess Luna! She taught me that one of the best things you can do with friendship is to give it to others and help them find it themselves! And I'm happy to report that all of Ponyville has learned that even if somepony seems a little intimidating, even scary, when you offer them your friendship, you'll discover a whole new pony underneath. And even if my Star Swirl the Bearded costume didn't go over, this still turned out to be the best Nightmare Night ever!
—Twilight Sparkle

Sisterhooves Social

Rarity wakes up to find her parents are going off on a vacation, leaving her little sister, Sweetie Belle, with her for the week. The clumsy Sweetie Belle immediately starts creating problems for Rarity, ruining the perfectionism of her lifestyle. Discouraged, Sweetie Belle seeks the counsel of Apple Bloom, who tells her about the Sisterhooves Social, an event especially for sisters that might bring the two back together. However, when Rarity refuses to attend, the two sisters decide they would be better off without each other and "un-sister."

Sweetie Belle spends time with Apple Bloom and Applejack, wishing she had the kind of sisterly love that they shared. Meanwhile, Rarity finds that all of Sweetie Belle's little mishaps have actually turned out to be good things and regrets her mistreatment of Sweetie Belle. She grovels at the feet of her little sister, who refuses the apology. Applejack tries to tell Rarity that being a sister is about give-and-take, not simply taking.

Sweetie Belle attends the Sisterhooves Social with Applejack and Apple Bloom. She runs a sister race with Applejack, and when they make it to the end, Applejack's hat falls off, revealing a horn—Rarity had costumed herself like Applejack and ran the whole race with Sweetie Belle! Applejack and Apple Bloom had been in on the plan the whole time. Rarity and Sweetie Belle make up and agree that, while it isn't always easy, having a sister truly is one of the best kinds of friendship.

FRIENDSHIP LESSON:

Dear Princess Celestia,

I agree that being sisters is a wonderful thing, but it takes teamwork. Sometimes it's about compromising. Sometimes it's about accepting each other's differences. But mostly, it's about having fun together. Even if it means getting your hooves a medium amount of dirty, not too little, not too much, just right.

—Rarity and Sweetie Belle

The Cutie Pox

though Apple Bloom and her Cutie Mark Crusaders try everything to get their marks, nothing works. Apple Bloom becomes extremely discouraged. During a visit with Zecora, she wonders if one of Zecora's potions will give her a cutie mark. Zecora warns that time is the only way for a cutie mark to appear, but when she leaves to gather ingredients, Apple Bloom takes a flower called Heart's Desire, convinced it will help her find her talent and cutie mark.

Apple Bloom arrives at school the next day with a loop-de-hoop cutie mark and displays her talents. Before long, *another* cutie mark appears—spinning plates—and she performs that simultaneously with her hooping. That night, a *third* mark appears—tap dancing shoes—and

Apple Bloom performs all three talents, which now seem to be out of her control.

After consulting with Twilight, Apple Bloom learns she has Cutie Pox, a rare pony disease that causes random cutie marks to appear and forces the pony to perform all the talents that come to her indefinitely. More and more cutie marks keep appearing on Apple Bloom, so the ponies rush to Zecora, who plants a special seed to cure Apple Bloom that will grow only when she tells the truth. Apple Bloom admits her cutie marks are fake. She learns that, while waiting for something can be really hard, trying to take a shortcut never works out the way you want it to. Good things come to those who wait.

FRIENDSHIP LESSON:

Dear Princess Celestia.
Waiting for what your heart desires can be really hard. So, you may try to take a shortcut. But this dishonesty never works, because you didn't earn what your heart desired. The only cure is being honest with yourself and others. And that's something every heart desires.

—Apple Bloom

EPISODE 207

May the Best Pet Win!

W hen Rainbow Dash discovers that her best friends get together for a weekly "Pet Playdate" with all their pets, she decides she will get a pet, too. Fluttershy takes Rainbow Dash to her cottage to choose a new companion that meets her requirements of "awesome" and "cool." In an epic song sequence, they consider many different options, eventually deciding to hold a contest to find out which pet will be best for Rainbow Dash.

At the initial lineup for the pet competition, Rainbow Dash finds a tortoise among the bunch and, despite her better judgment, agrees to let him compete. She tests the pets on speed, agility, guts, style, "coolness," "awesomeness," and "radicalness." The tortoise fails at everything and Rainbow Dash lets him know how lame she thinks he is. The final round is a race through Ghastly Gorge against the Pegasus herself.

During the race, Rainbow Dash accidentally causes an avalanche and finds herself trapped beneath a rock. The competitors take no notice and fly on, leaving only the tortoise to help her. She ultimately chooses the tortoise as her new pet, realizing that there are more important qualities in a friend than being cool. She names her pet Tank and gives him a propeller so he can fly around with her.

FRIENDSHIP LESSON:

Dear Princess Celestia,
I used to think that the most important traits to look for in a pet, or any best friend, were all physical competitive abilities. But now I can see how shortsighted and shallow that was. Today I learned what the most important quality really is. A certain kind of spirit. A stick-to-it-ive-ness. A never give up, can-do attitude that's the mark of a real winner. And this tortoise has it.
                              —Rainbow Dash

The Mysterious Mare Do Well

R ainbow Dash has become the hero of Ponyville, constantly saving everypony from harm. While her friends are proud of her, they believe the fame is going to her head. Soon, a new cloaked hero swoops in and steals the spotlight. The mysterious pony leaves without revealing her identity, and the mayor declares this "Mysterious Mare Do Well" to be Ponyville's new hero.

Rainbow Dash is constantly one-upped by Mare Do Well and grows increasingly frustrated, especially when her friends start to fawn over the new hero as well. She sets out to prove that she really is better than this new hero. Her unsuccessful attempts at defending her title sink her into an even deeper funk, worsened by the fact that her fan club diverts their attention to Mare Do Well.

In a jealous rage, Rainbow Dash tries to unmask Mare Do Well at a parade being held in Mare Do Well's honor. The result is a chase scene that reveals there is more than one Mare Do Well. Rainbow catches the multiple ponies and, upon unmasking them, learns that her friends— Pinkie Pie, Twilight Sparkle, and Applejack—have been posing as the new hero at different times. They explain their motive was to teach Rainbow Dash the importance of grace and humility. Rainbow comes to understand that she needs to be considerate of others in her heroism and give others credit when they outshine her in certain tasks.

FRIENDSHIP LESSON:

What we're trying to say is, it's great to be really good at something, but it's important to act with grace and humility.

—Twilight Sparkle

EPISODE 209

Sweet and Elite

Rarity is going to Canterlot to select new materials for her fashion designs—but this is a special trip because Twilight Sparkle has arranged for her to stay at the castle as a guest of Princess Celestia! In the spirit of generosity, Rarity plans to thank Twilight by designing an exquisite birthday dress for her. While shopping in Canterlot, Rarity is acutely aware that her humble origins in Ponyville are looked down upon by these high-society ponies. However, her personal connection to the princess impresses Fancypants, a fashionable pony at the very top of the upper crust.

Fancypants invites Rarity to watch the Wonderbolts Derby from his VIP seats. Although it will take time away from designing Twilight's birthday present, Rarity simply can't pass up the chance to become accepted by the capital's elite tastemakers. Desperate to fit in, she begins making up stories about her background and quickly becomes so in demand that her social calendar leaves no time for her to attend Twilight's birthday party at all. Rarity writes a letter to Twilight, lying that her cat, Opal, is sick, so Rarity will have to miss the party.

The next day, her five friends show up at her castle suite—to Rarity's horror, they have brought the party to her! Now Rarity runs the risk of being caught in two lies, so to save face, she runs back and forth between the two competing groups of friends. When her Ponyville friends crash the high-society party, Rarity is mortified, but to her surprise, Fancypants takes a liking to them as well, and Rarity realizes how wrong she has been. She apologizes for all her insincerity and learns that you should always be proud of where you come from.

FRIENDSHIP LESSON:

Dear Princess Celestia,
I wanted to tell you about the important lesson I learned during my visit. I learned that no matter where you go in life, you should never forget that you are the product of your home and your friends. And that is something always to be proud of, no matter what.
                                                    —Rarity

Secret of My Excess

Spike had been saving a precious fire ruby for his birthday dinner, but when he sees how much Rarity admires it, he gives it to her, deeming the generous action totally worth the kiss on the cheek that he receives. On Spike's birthday, the ponies shower him with affection and presents. He begins milking the day for all it is worth, demanding gifts from everyone he comes across in Ponyville.

The next day, when Spike wakes up, he is grabbier than ever and seems to have accelerated through adolescence overnight, now sporting a deep voice and having grown twice his original size. Zecora explains to Twilight that Spike is growing up, and the bigger dragons get, the greedier they get. They need to find a way to keep Spike from being so greedy. Soon, Spike is completely out of control, growing bigger by the second and plundering Ponyville. Twilight Sparkle enlists the help of her friends to stop him, but to no avail.

Spike kidnaps Rarity, but she does not realize the dragon is Spike. When he eyes her fire-ruby necklace, she refuses to give it to him, telling the story of how it was given to her. Spike suddenly remembers his past and shrinks back to his normal size in midair. Though he and Rarity almost plummet to their deaths, they are saved by Fluttershy and Rainbow Dash.

FRIENDSHIP LESSON:

Dear Princess Celestia,

Today I learned a great lesson about friendship. Well, you might think that it would feel good to get lots and lots of stuff, but it doesn't feel nearly as good as giving something special to somepony you really care about. But I learned that it truly is better to give than to receive and that kindness and generosity are what lead to true friendship. And that's more valuable than anything in the world. Well... almost anything.

—Spike

Hearth's Warming Eve

Hearth's Warming Eve is Equestria's most celebrated winter holiday, and it is tradition for ponies to act out a play that illustrates the origin of the holiday. Princess Celestia invites Twilight Sparkle and her Ponyville friends to Canterlot to star in the pageant about the founding of Equestria.

The story reenacts how Unicorns, Pegasi, and Earth Ponies were once at odds with one another, arguing and fighting over petty things. Their cold behavior toward one another was causing a perpetual winter, making it hard for them to survive. A meeting among the leaders of each tribe did not resolve their differences. The tribes decided to find a new land to populate separately. After much searching, they each settled in the land of Equestria—paradise, or so they thought. The tribes argued about whom the land belonged to, each claiming to have found it first.

As the bickering continued, a group of Windigos appeared. The winter spirits feed off of fighting and hatred and were drawn by the tension among the three tribe leaders. The leaders realized that their behavior had destroyed this once pristine land as well. They agreed to try to put aside their differences and claim the land together. The power of their newfound friendship restored the land, which they shared forever after!

FRIENDSHIP LESSON:

We brought this blizzard to our home by fightin' and not trustin' each other. Now it's destroyin' this land, too.
—Applejack
(as Smart Cookie)

And now our bodies will become as cold as our hearts... all because we were foolish enough to hate.
—Twilight Sparkle
(as Clover the Clever)

Family Appreciation Day

A pple Bloom is very excited to partake in her family's annual tradition of making their zap apple jam. Granny Smith has just begun to show her the unique and awkward process when Silver Spoon and Diamond Tiara peek in on the Apple family and begin taunting Apple Bloom about her silly grandmother. To make matters worse, Apple Bloom must bring Granny to school for Family Appreciation Day the following week, and she fears she will become a laughingstock.

Apple Bloom's Cutie Mark Crusader friends try to help her find a way to keep Granny from making an appearance at school on Monday for the presentation—from faking illness to trying to jumpstart the zap apple harvest to pretending to cancel the presentation. Despite their best efforts, Granny arrives on time for the presentation Monday morning.

Granny surprises everyone by telling an amazing story about her youth, in which there was no Ponyville. Her father, an avid apple seed collector, was granted his land near the Everfree Forest by Princess Celestia herself. As a young filly, Granny ventured into the forest and discovered the magical zap apple trees and learned the proper techniques to harvest them and make them into jam. Her success with the jam led to the founding of Ponyville. In fact, Diamond Tiara's great-grandfather Stinkin' Rich got his start in business selling Granny's jam.

The class is impressed. Apple Bloom realizes that she should have known how special her family truly is all along. She apologizes to Granny, and together they carry out another successful zap apple season.

FRIENDSHIP LESSON:

My Granny Smith is super special! I just forgot that for a little while.
—Apple Bloom

EPISODE 213

Baby Cakes

twilight and her friends are excited for the birth of Mr. and Mrs. Cake's twin foals, especially Pinkie Pie, who can't wait to play with them! Pound Cake, a boy Pegasus, and Pumpkin Cake, a girl Unicorn, love Pinkie Pie, and they spend all their time together laughing and playing, pausing only to be fed, burped, and changed. But when the overworked Mr. and Mrs. Cake need a last-minute foal-sitter, they don't consider Pinkie Pie, because she doesn't seem to take responsibility seriously. Pinkie Pie desperately wants to foal-sit and convinces them that she is plenty responsible for the job. When nopony else is available, the Cakes nervously agree.

Pinkie Pie soon discovers that there is a lot more to foal-sitting than fun and games, and before long, she finds herself in way over her head as the twins prove to be very mischievous. When Twilight shows up at her door, Pinkie is relieved, but then Twilight makes a comment implying Pinkie isn't cut out for the responsibility. Determined to prove she can handle the twins on her own, Pinkie finally succeeds in getting the twins to fall asleep for their nap, but the second she looks away, the twins disappear.

The twins' magic powers are spiraling out of control, allowing them to evade Pinkie's "responsible" grasp. Pound Cake flies around the room while Pumpkin Cake uses her Unicorn powers to enchant her toys. When the twins see how distraught they have made Pinkie Pie, they settle down and turn the tables, attempting to make *her* laugh instead.

FRIENDSHIP LESSON:

Dear Princess Celestia,
I've always had fun playing with little kids and I thought babysitting meant just more playtime, right? Wrong! Being a caregiver is way more responsibility than just being a playmate, and today I learned that sometimes our desire for responsibility can outrun our actual ability to handle it.
—Pinkie Pie

The Last Roundup

W hen Ponyville's Town Hall's roof caves in, the Ponyvillians put their faith in Applejack to help them fix it. Applejack has entered the National Rodeo Competition and has promised to donate her winnings to fix Town Hall. The town sends her off with parties, fully expecting Applejack to sweep the competition. However, the day Applejack is expected to return home, her friends receive a letter saying simply, "Not coming back to Ponyville. Don't worry. Will send money soon."

The five friends leave Ponyville to search for Applejack, eventually finding her in Dodge Junction working on a cherry orchard for Cherry

Jubilee. The girls pry Applejack about her reasons for not coming home, but she is very secretive and defensive. The next day, all five friends show up at the cherry orchard and report that they, too, have been hired. They spend their time pressing Applejack for answers but get nothing except a bad attitude.

The friends get their hopes up when Applejack promises to tell them the truth at breakfast the next morning. But when the time comes, they find that Applejack has fled! After a high-speed chase, they catch Applejack, and she spills the beans. Though she won plenty of ribbons at the rodeo, none of them were for first place. She was ashamed and couldn't face Ponyville until she'd earned some money to help fix Town Hall, so she took the cherry orchard job. The girls tell her how much they love her anyway, and that all that matters to them is that she tried her best.

FRIENDSHIP LESSON:

Dear Princess Celestia,
It's a tad easier to be proud when you come in first than it is when you finish further back. But there's no reason to hide when you don't do as well as you'd hoped. You can't run away from your problems. Better to run to your friends and family.

—Applejack

The Super Speedy Cider Squeezy 6000

Sweet Apple Acres struggles to keep up with demand during cider season. Every year, the taps run dry and would-be customers get agitated, especially Rainbow Dash. But the Apple family refuses to compromise on the quality of their product in the interest of quantity. Out of nowhere, two Unicorn brothers, Flim and Flam, ride into Sweet Apple Acres on a strange machine. They burst into a theatrical song and dance, pitching their new cider-squeezing device to the Apple family's thirsty patrons. The Apples refuse to buy into the scheme, and the Flim Flam brothers threaten to put them out of business by becoming their sole cider competitor.

When the Flim Flam brothers return the next morning, they challenge the Apple family to a contest: Whoever can make the most cider wins the exclusive right to sell cider in Ponyville. If the Apples don't win the competition, they will lose their farm, because cider sales are their cash cow. Applejack and her friends are confident in Sweet Apple Acres's ability to beat out the scheming Unicorns, but once the competition begins, the brothers immediately begin outproducing the Apples.

With help from Twilight and the girls, Applejack's team is able to pull ahead. But the devious brothers aren't ready to give up. They decide to forgo quality control, putting bad apples, even twigs and bark, into their cider. At the end of the competition, the Flim Flam brothers have produced more barrels of cider, but their product is so unpalatable that everypony refuses to buy it. Seeing they've lost Ponyville's business, the brothers move on to the next town.

FRIENDSHIP LESSON:

Dear Princess Celestia,

I wanted to share my thoughts with you. I didn't learn anythin'! Ha! I was right all along! If you take your time to do things the right way, your work will speak for itself. Sure, I could tell you I learned somethin' about how my friends are always there to help me and I can count on them no matter what, but truth is, I knew that already, too.

—Applejack

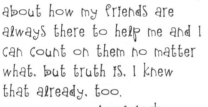

EPISODE 216

Read It and Weep

R ainbow Dash suffers a flying accident that lands her in Ponyville Hospital for a few days. When Twilight Sparkle brings her a book to read, Rainbow Dash refuses—reading is decidedly "uncool." Twilight goes on to describe the book's heroine, Daring Do, who sounds a lot like Rainbow Dash. Still, Rainbow Dash refuses. But as the minutes drag on, all other attempts to amuse herself fail and she picks up the book. Once Rainbow Dash allows herself to admit that she loves the story, she is totally hooked and can't put the book down!

In an effort to cheer her up, Twilight and Fluttershy visit Rainbow Dash, unaware they're keeping her from the world of *Daring Do and the Quest for the Sapphire Stone*. Rainbow Dash tries every excuse to get them to leave so she can return to the exciting plot twists. The next morning, Rainbow Dash is finally discharged from the hospital. But instead of being relieved, she is dismayed because she has left the book behind in her hospital room. She has to find a way back in there!

When Rainbow Dash fails at her attempts to get readmitted to the hospital, she sneaks in after dark to steal it back, causing a ruckus in Ponyville. With no choice but to admit her real motive, she confesses that she loves the book and loves reading! She has learned that reading is something anypony can enjoy, and just because you're athletic doesn't mean you can't be a bookworm, too.

FRiENDSHiP LESSoN:

I shouldn't knock something until I've tried it.

—Rainbow Dash

Hearts and Hooves Day

t he Cutie Mark Crusaders are celebrating Hearts and Hooves Day. They present their teacher, Miss Cheerilee, with a special card and ask her if she has a "special somepony" to celebrate with. When she says no, they are in disbelief and set out to find her a stallion. One adorable song sequence later, Sweetie Belle decides that Big Mac, Apple Bloom and Applejack's big brother, is the perfect match.

The Cutie Mark Crusaders set up a romantic lunch for the pair, but it ends up being an awkward mess. When that doesn't work, they mix up a batch of love potion and trick Cheerilee and Big Mac into drinking it. This seems to work—Cheerilee asks Big Mac to be her special somepony and he accepts! The Crusaders are ecstatic until it works a little too well. Cheerilee and Big Mac are acting so over-the-top sappy that everypony else can hardly stand it.

Apple Bloom fears she may have accidentally given them love *poison* that got them lost in each other's eyes to the point that they forget to pay attention to their responsibilities. The antidote is to keep the two from looking into each other's eyes for a full hour. The three fillies tell Cheerilee and Big Mac they must spend the day preparing for their wedding in the hopes that it will buy them some time. They manage to keep the two apart for the whole hour, and Cheerilee and Big Mac snap out of their romance trance. The Crusaders admit what happened to Cheerilee and learn a valuable lesson.

FRIENDSHIP LESSON:

It's up to everypony to choose that very special somepony for themselves.
—Sweetie Belle

A Friend in Deed

Everypony loves Pinkie Pie, and she loves nothing more than making ponies smile! She knows everything about every Ponyvillian and just how to make them happy. So when grumpy Cranky Doodle Donkey comes rolling into town, Pinkie is right there to welcome him and brighten his day! Only he doesn't want to be welcomed or have his day brightened, and he certainly doesn't want to make friends with Pinkie Pie.

Pinkie continues to try to befriend Cranky. She treats him to a day at the spa, which softens him a bit, but he won't crack a smile. He heads off to unpack his things, and Pinkie follows along to help. Cranky reveals that he has traveled all over Equestria, hinting at the fact that he was looking for somepony in particular, but Pinkie doesn't pick up on this. She accidentally ruins a photo album of his, and he sends her away. He will never, ever befriend her.

Pinkie tries to apologize, but Cranky rebuffs her, saying she ruined the only thing he had left to remember "her" by. Pinkie pieces it all together and returns later with a guest—Matilda, another donkey. Upon seeing her, Cranky smiles, and it turns out that the two are long-lost loves. He thanks Pinkie for reuniting him with Matilda and accepts her friendship.

FRIENDSHIP LESSON:

Dear Princess Celestia,
There are many different kinds of friends and many ways to express friendship. Some friends like to run and laugh and play together. But others just like to be left alone, and that's fine, too. But the best thing about friendship is being able to make your friends smile.

—Pinkie Pie

Putting Your Hoof Down

While feeding her critter friends, Fluttershy encounters a problem: Angel Bunny refuses to eat anything she gives him. He demands a very special meal. When Fluttershy goes out to buy the ingredients, she is constantly taken advantage of by the vendors and other ponies, so Rarity and Pinkie Pie swoop in to help her learn to assert herself. Fluttershy vows to stop being such a pushover.

Fluttershy attends a seminar on standing up for yourself taught by self-help guru Iron Will. He has a tough-guy attitude and refuses to let anyone mess with him. After the assertiveness training seminar,

Fluttershy starts implementing these new techniques and gets instant results. But she becomes so rude and pushy in her attempts to stop being a pushover that even her friends admit they miss Old Fluttershy, who was polite and considerate.

Fluttershy takes her assertiveness too far when she insults Rarity and Pinkie Pie. Upon seeing how upset she's made them, Fluttershy feels sorry. But she isn't done standing up for herself. Iron Will eventually comes to collect his payment from Fluttershy, and she calmly tells him she was dissatisfied with his program and won't pay. She learns that standing up for yourself doesn't mean you have to change who you are. You can be kind *and* assertive.

FRIENDSHIP LESSON:

Dear Princess Celestia,
Sometimes it can be hard for a shy pony like me to stand up for myself. And when I first tried it, I didn't like the pony I became. But I learned that standing up for yourself isn't the same as changing who you are. Now I know how to put my hoof down without being unpleasant or mean.
—Fluttershy

EPISODE 220

It's About Time

While trying to schedule time to create a schedule, Twilight Sparkle is visited by a version of herself from the future! Future Twilight looks like she's been through a disaster. She tries to issue a dire warning to Present Twilight but is sucked back into the space-time vortex before she can finish. Twilight deduces that some major disaster must have befallen Equestria and spends the next few days trying to disaster-proof Ponyville.

Despite Twilight Sparkle's best efforts, it looks like the future is unfolding in the same manner that caused Future Twilight to bear a scar, crazy haircut, bandage, and eye patch. Twilight becomes frantic, realizing that she's failing at preventing the future, and tries even harder to put off the inevitable.

174

The only solution seems to be a spell to time-travel into the future, but Twilight and her friends can't find one before the morning of Future Twilight's vague warning. To everypony's surprise, no disaster occurs. Twilight realizes she had been worrying over nothing and should have let the future handle itself. She learns that Future Twilight was only trying to warn her not to worry so much!

FRiENDSHiP LESSON:

Dear Princess Celestia,
I couldn't stop worrying and let the future handle itself! Well, not anymore. From now on, I'm gonna solve problems as they come and stop worrying about every little thing!

               —Twilight Sparkle

EPISODE 221

Dragon Quest

he six Ponyville friends gather to watch the Great Dragon Migration, which only happens once in a generation. Rainbow Dash comments on how unlike the other dragons Spike is. This prompts Spike to start questioning his identity. What does it mean to be a dragon and how does he fit in? He embarks on a quest to find the answers by joining the Great Dragon Migration. His concerned friends—Twilight Sparkle, Rainbow Dash, and Rarity—decide to follow him and keep an eye on him from afar.

Spike meets a group of teenage dragons, and when they find out he lives in Ponyville, they challenge him to prove his dragonhood through a series of tests. Twilight, Rainbow Dash, and Rarity, disguised as a giant dragon, step in to ensure no serious trouble befalls Spike in any activity, though he is still unsuccessful in all of them. Once they let him take on a challenge on his own, he earns the respect of the other dragons. The leader of the gang, Garble, accepts Spike into the group.

Spike is thrilled until they start terrorizing animals around them, trying to steal phoenix eggs and encouraging Spike to destroy the eggs. He stands up to the dragon gang and refuses. They're about to retaliate when the ponies reveal themselves and step in. They save Spike and return to Ponyville. Spike writes the princess a letter saying he learned that *what* you are does not dictate *who* you are and he is very happy to live in Ponyville. Spike even gets a new friend out of his adventure—a baby phoenix he names Peewee.

FRIENDSHIP LESSON:

Dear Princess Celestia,
Seeing the Great Dragon Migration made me wonder what it meant to be a dragon. But now I realize that who I am is not the same as what I am. I may have been born a dragon, but Equestria and my pony friends have taught me how to be kind, loyal, and true. I'm proud to call Ponyville my home and to have my pony friends as my family.
Yours truly,
Spike

EPISODE 222

Hurricane Fluttershy

E ach year, Pegasus ponies must send a supply of water to
Cloudsdale so new clouds and rain can be distributed around
Equestria during the rainy season. This year, Ponyville has been
chosen to provide all the rainwater for Equestria. Rainbow Dash
recruits every Pegasus in Ponyville, including Fluttershy, to collectively
create a tornado powerful enough to send water up into the clouds
to last a whole year. Fluttershy is convinced she can't do it but finally
agrees to help when Rainbow tells her this will earn the respect of the
Wonderbolts.

It's almost time to get to work when Rainbow Dash measures everypony's wingpower. Fluttershy is humiliated when she only measures a .5 out of 10. Determined to help her friend Rainbow Dash, she trains and grows stronger but only improves to 2.3 wingpower. She backs out of the tornado-making event. However, on the big day, eight members of Rainbow Dash's crew are sick and the remaining Pegasi cannot generate enough wingpower to raise the water up into the clouds.

Fluttershy appears in the nick of time and, encouraged by her friends, joins the fight. Finally, with her help, the Pegasi reach optimum wingpower and the water funnels up off the ground. Fluttershy has saved the day!

FRIENDSHIP LESSON:

Dear Princess Celestia,
Sometimes you can feel like what you have to offer is too little to make a difference, but today I learned that everypony's contribution is important no matter how small. If you just keep your head high, do your best, and believe in yourself, anything can happen!
—Fluttershy

EPISODE 223

Ponyville Confidential

t he Cutie Mark Crusaders join the school newspaper in another attempt to earn their marks. They find it hard to please editor Diamond Tiara, and none of their hard work in journalism is appreciated. Diamond Tiara wants juicy stories, and when they finally write a gossip column about Snips and Snails, it seems to earn her respect. She asks them to continue writing the gossip column under the pen name "Gabby Gums," and the fillies set out to find more "news."

When all of Ponyville starts talking about the new Gabby Gums column, the Ponyvillians find it amusing at first. But the Gabby Gums trio takes the stories too far when they target Twilight Sparkle and her five best friends. When Rarity's private diary ends up in the column, the six friends realize it must be Sweetie Belle's doing.

With Gabby Gums's true identity revealed, Sweetie Belle, Scootaloo, and Apple Bloom are ashamed, and none of their friends will accept their apologies. Diamond Tiara wants them to continue writing the column, threatening to blackmail them with embarrassing photos if they refuse to comply. It's time for the Cutie Mark Crusaders to come up with a plan. They write one last column, an open letter to Ponyville, issuing an apology and explaining how their desire to earn cutie marks spiraled out of control. They realize that their friends are far more important than earning their cutie marks.

FRIENDSHIP LESSON:

To the citizens of Ponyville,

For some time now, you've been reading this column to get the latest dirt and the hottest buzz. But this will be my final piece. We want to apologize for the pain and embarrassment we've caused. Y'see, I'm actually three little fillies, Sweetie Belle, Apple Bloom, and Scootaloo. As the popularity of our column grew, we got swept up in the hype. We knew that what we were doing didn't feel quite right, but we ignored the guilt because everypony seemed to want to read what we were writing. From now on, we promise to respect everypony else's privacy, and we won't engage in hurtful gossip anymore. All we can do is ask for your forgiveness, Ponyville.

Signing off for the very last time, xoxo,

Gabby Gums

MMMystery on the Friendship Express

Pinkie Pie has been entrusted with the safe delivery of Mr. and Mrs. Cake's towering entry in the National Dessert Competition: the Marzipan Mascarpone Meringue Madness! She enlists all her friends to help escort the cake on the train to Canterlot. Several other bakers are also on the train, all determined that their dessert will win. Pinkie keeps watch over her charge throughout the night, but suspicious things keep happening. The next morning, she sees that someone has been nibbling on the desserts—all the entries are ruined!

Pinkie Pie carries out a wild investigation of the competitors,

Gustave Le Grand, Donut Joe, and Mulia Mild. Logical Twilight Sparkle disproves all of Pinkie's hypotheses. When the lights go out again, even more cake-gobbling is heard. The culprit is still out there!

With Twilight's help, Pinkie concludes that the cake saboteurs are none other than Applejack, Fluttershy, Rarity, and Rainbow Dash—and she's right! They ashamedly admit that Pinkie made the cake sound so delicious that they all snuck a few bites. It is then revealed that the other bakers had been nibbling on one another's treats as well. Now, having no desserts to enter into the contest, the group works together to remake their masterpieces.

FRIENDSHIP LESSON:

Dear Princess Celestia,

Today I learned that it's not good to jump to conclusions. You have to find out all the facts before saying somepony did something. If you don't, you could end up blaming somepony for something they never did. This could hurt their feelings. And it could make you feel really foolish. So from now on, I will always make sure to get all the facts.

—Pinkie Pie

EPISODE 225

A Canterlot Wedding, Part 1

S pike delivers a scroll from Princess Celestia announcing that a
wedding is soon to take place in Canterlot and the six friends
all have special jobs in the wedding preparations. The invitation
reads that Princess Mi Amore Cadenza is marrying Shining Armor,
Twilight Sparkle's brother. Twilight is furious and hurt that her own
big brother did not tell her the news himself. However, she sets aside
her disappointment as the ponies depart for Canterlot.

When the girls arrive, Twilight Sparkle gives Shining Armor a piece
of her mind. He explains that he had been so focused on a current threat

to Canterlot, and as captain of the Royal Guard, all his energy had gone into protective spells surrounding the city. He then reveals that his bride-to-be is Princess Cadance, Twilight's old foal-sitter. Twilight is overjoyed at first, but her excitement ends when she sees how rude Cadance is to all her friends, not appreciating their hard work on the wedding. None of the other ponies seems to notice, and Twilight feels very alone in her dislike for Cadance.

Twilight tries to pay a visit to her brother when she witnesses Cadance putting a seemingly evil spell on him. This isn't the Cadance she remembers—and worse, Cadance doesn't even seem to remember Twilight at all, not even the secret hoof-shake they once shared. Twilight feels there's only one thing to do—interrupt the wedding rehearsal and declare Cadance to be evil! Shining Armor makes excuses for his bride as he and all the ponies leave Twilight alone to regret the scene she has caused. Suddenly, Cadance appears, and before Twilight can really apologize, Cadance gets a nasty look in her eye. In a flash of green light, the two ponies disappear.

EPISODE 226

A Canterlot Wedding, Part 2

twilight awakens imprisoned in a cave of sparkling crystals. Evil Cadance has teleported her, then trapped her there! While attempting to free herself from imprisonment, Twilight spots Cadance, and a battle ensues. Twilight finally overcomes her, but oddly, Cadance begs Twilight for mercy. Cadance then explains that she is the real Cadance, and the evil mare who trapped both of them in the crystal cave is actually an imposter. Real Cadance proves her identity by performing their old secret hoof-shake with Twilight. The two team up to try to escape, hoping to stop the wedding before anything terrible happens to Shining Armor. But Imposter Cadance is already walking down the aisle!

Real Cadance and Twilight Sparkle burst into the wedding, exposing the imposter, but are they too late? Shining Armor remains under a spell and seems not to notice the commotion. Impostor Cadance sheds her innocent facade and reveals herself to be a changeling! Her real name is Queen Chrysalis, and she gains power by feeding off of one pony's love for another. By harnessing Shining Armor's love for Princess Cadance, Chrysalis has already gained enough power to bring her hordes of changeling minions to Equestria. When Princess Celestia is unable to defeat Queen Chrysalis, she calls upon the six ponies to use the Elements of Harmony to stop her.

The ponies are captured before they can retrieve the Elements, but the real Cadance has a backup plan. She breaks Shining Armor out of his trance and tells him to perform his protection spell again. Cadance combines his magic with her own, which proves powerful enough to defeat Queen Chrysalis and her army of minions. Princess Celestia congratulates Twilight for trusting her instincts and saving the day. With the changelings gone, nothing remains but the happy celebrations of the *real* wedding.

FRIENDSHIP LESSON:

Learning to trust your instincts is a valuable lesson to learn.
—Princess Celestia

The Crystal Empire, Part 1

In Canterlot, Princess Celestia receives a warning from a royal guard: "It has returned." She summons Twilight Sparkle to Canterlot at once, explaining that Twilight will have to find a way to protect the Crystal Empire, a part of Equestria that vanished into thin air a thousand years ago and has just reappeared. The Empire is under immediate threat from a dark Unicorn named King Sombra, who once cursed the Empire, causing its disappearance. Twilight and her Ponyville friends are to join Shining Armor and Princess Cadance in the Crystal Empire and work together to find a solution. Before Twilight leaves, Princess

Celestia tells her that in order to move on to the next level of her studies, it must be Twilight alone who ultimately succeeds in saving the Empire.

The Friendship Express takes the six ponies and Spike north from Canterlot to the icy tundra on the outskirts of the Crystal Empire, where Shining Armor is there to greet them. As they race through the harsh landscape toward the safety of the Empire, they are followed by a massive shadowy figure that is closing in on the shimmering city. Shining Armor stands his ground against the dark, looming Unicorn figure and successfully protects the ponies, though his horn is corrupted in the fight. Once safely inside the Crystal Castle, the ponies see that Princess Cadance isn't doing so well. She has been using her magic to keep King Sombra out of the Crystal Empire, but it is draining her strength.

The ponies spread out across the Crystal Empire to gather information from the Crystal ponies, but nopony can remember anything from before King Sombra's rise to power. Maybe they will find some clues in the Crystal Library! They comb the stacks and finally find *History of the Crystal Empire*, which tells of an annual festival called the Crystal Faire that served to renew the spirit of love and unity in the Empire, protecting it from harm. They meticulously re-create all the elements of the fair. As the Crystal ponies enter the festival, the plan seems to work! Memories of the prosperous era before King Sombra come flooding back. And the ponies are eager to see the fair's main attraction, the Crystal Heart. But the original Crystal Heart was endowed with a magic that channeled the happiness of the ponies into protection for the Empire. The replica the ponies made isn't magical at all, and without the original, their plan will fail. Twilight believes she has to be the one to restore the Crystal Heart. *That* must be what Princess Celestia's final words in Canterlot meant.

The Crystal Empire, Part 2

While Twilight Sparkle and Spike are searching the Crystal Castle for the Crystal Heart, their Ponyville friends are carrying out the traditional Crystal Faire activities. If the Crystal ponies suspect that anything is wrong with the Crystal Heart, their spirits will be crushed, and darkness will surely consume the Empire again. Twilight uncovers a hidden staircase and descends to find an enchanted door. Upon opening it, she is transported to a very strange place—a place where she is faced with her worst fear. Princess Celestia is there, and she tells Twilight she has failed her test and can no longer continue as Celestia's student, coldly dismissing her. Luckily, Spike arrives on the scene to find Twilight frozen in a trance and snaps her back into the present. Twilight realizes her nightmare was part of King Sombra's dark magic and uses her own magic to advance beyond the scary door. Meanwhile, at the fair, the horrified Crystal ponies finally uncover the phony Heart. While Applejack and Rarity try to calm the crowd, Twilight and Spike arrive at the real Crystal Heart at the very top of the castle. But as Twilight reaches for it, sharp black crystals shoot up from the floor, trapping her in a crystal prison. It was booby-trapped by King Sombra!

Twilight knows there is only one way to save the Empire now: Spike must be the one to reunite the Crystal ponies with the Crystal Heart, even if it means she will fail Celestia's test. In a dramatic escape from King Sombra, Spike manages to get the Heart into Princess Cadance's hooves, and with her last ounce of strength, Cadance and the Crystal ponies activate its protective properties. The Crystal Empire is saved!

Back in Canterlot, Princess Celestia commends Twilight for her decision. Self-sacrifice for the interest of others is what allowed her to *pass* the test.

FRiENDSHiP LESSoN:

Twilight, as I understand it, Spike brought Princess Cadance the Crystal Heart because you weren't sure how quickly you could find a way to escape the tower. You weren't willing to risk the future of the citizens of the Crystal Empire in an effort to guarantee your own. Far better that I have a student who understands the meaning of self-sacrifice than one who only looks out for her own best interests.

—Princess Celestia

EPISODE 303

Too Many Pinkie Pies

When Applejack invites Pinkie Pie to a barn raising and Rainbow Dash invites her to play at the swimming hole at the same time, Pinkie hatches a plan to duplicate herself at the Mirror Pool so she doesn't have to miss out on any of the fun. Once her clone is made, Pinkie instructs the new Pinkie to attend the barn raising while she hangs out with Rainbow Dash. The plan seems to be working...until the new Pinkie runs into Fluttershy, who has yet another fun offer. The clone does not know which event to choose.

Pinkie's clone tells the real Pinkie about this new dilemma. Pinkie then decides that the only solution is to make more duplicates. However, these new duplicates then use the Mirror Pool to make even *more* Pinkies. Soon Ponyville is overrun with Pinkies. They are making everything decidedly *not* fun for all involved. Twilight Sparkle does some research and discovers a spell that will send the duplicates back into the Mirror Pool. However, there is a catch: The friends must identify the original Pinkie Pie, or they risk sending her back into the pool, too.

Twilight and her friends devise a test to find the real Pinkie Pie, and they corral all the Pinkies in Ponyville. Twilight knows that the real Pinkie will do anything for her friends, so she instructs all the Pinkies to sit still while watching paint dry on a wall. Whichever Pinkie stays focused for the longest time will be allowed to stay, while anyone who gets distracted will be sent back into the pool. One by one, all the duplicate Pinkies are easily distracted. The real Pinkie, however, stands firm, determined to be reunited with her friends. When she is the last pony standing, she celebrates with her friends and writes to Celestia about the importance of having good friends over constant fun.

FRIENDSHIP LESSON:

Dear Princess Celestia,
It's great to have fun, but it's even greater to have great friends. And having lots of friends means that you sometimes have to make choices as to whom you'll spend your time with. But that's okay, because good friends will always give you lots of opportunities to have fun. So even if you're "missing out," it's never for long.

Respectfully yours,
Pinkie Pie

EPISODE 304

One Bad Apple

t he Apple family is preparing for the arrival of their cousin Babs
Seed from Manehattan. Apple Bloom is ecstatic to learn that Babs
is a "blank flank" just like herself, Sweetie Belle, and Scootaloo.
She hopes that Babs will join the Cutie Mark Crusaders. When Babs
arrives, things seem to be going well until Diamond Tiara and Silver
Spoon show up at the clubhouse and begin mocking the Cutie Mark
Crusaders. To Apple Bloom's dismay, Babs joins in, teasing the girls
and even ruining the float they have been working on for the Summer
Harvest Parade. Diamond Tiara, Silver Spoon, and Babs leave together,
warning the fillies not to be snitches.

Apple Bloom, Scootaloo, and Sweetie Belle fix up their float, making
it so beautiful that they *know* Babs will want to ride in it. They secretly

rig it so that it will go haywire while Babs is driving it. The Crusaders are rather pleased with themselves until Applejack comes along with a piece of unexpected news: Babs came to Ponyville to escape bullying over her "blank flank" back in Manehattan. The Crusaders realize their error in judgment, but Babs is already on the rigged float headed for disaster.

Apple Bloom selflessly pushes Babs out of harm's way, and the Crusaders apologize to Babs. She apologizes for her behavior, too, and becomes an official Cutie Mark Crusader. Babs heads back to Manehattan, promising to start a Cutie Mark Crusaders branch there as well.

FRIENDSHIP LESSON:

You see. Babs. we were tryin' to get you back for being a big bully.

—Apple Bloom

But then Applejack told us about how you were being bullied back in Manehattan.

—Scootaloo

And we figured out you were just doing it to avoid getting picked on in Ponyville. But by then we were the ones being bullies and—oh, why does life have to be so ironic?!

—Sweetie Belle

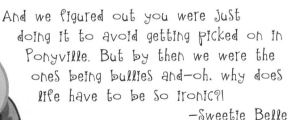

EPISODE 305

Magic Duel

he Great and Powerful Trixie returns to Ponyville to avenge her reputation since Twilight Sparkle humiliated her the last time she was in town. She challenges Twilight to a duel, which Twilight accepts only because Trixie promises to torment her friends with magic if she doesn't accept. Somehow, Trixie's magic has grown more powerful since their last encounter—even more powerful than Twilight's. Twilight loses the duel and is ejected from Ponyville, barred from reentry by a magical force field encapsulating Ponyville. Never one to accept defeat, Twilight vows to find a way back in.

Twilight gallops into the Everfree Forest and finds Zecora, who promises to teach her magic that will rival Trixie's. While Twilight is training under Zecora, her friends back in Ponyville are scouring

Golden Oak Library for answers. Within Twilight's bookshelves, they come across a picture of a necklace resembling the one Trixie wears. It is called the Alicorn Amulet, and it endows the wearer with untold powers but simultaneously corrupts them. The ponies know that with this information, Twilight could form a plan, so they elect Fluttershy to go into the forest to find her. With help from her critter friends, Fluttershy sneaks past the force field around Ponyville and reaches Twilight at Zecora's hut.

After completing intense magical training under Zecora, Twilight Sparkle challenges Trixie to a second duel; this time Twilight is sporting a green pendant that seems to rival the Alicorn Amulet. Trixie begrudgingly agrees, and to her surprise, Twilight performs the most beguiling magic Trixie has ever seen. Seething with envy, Trixie seizes Twilight's amulet for herself and relinquishes the Alicorn Amulet. In a surprising twist, Twilight reveals that her amulet is a fake! Her new magic tricks had been simple, nonmagical illusions made possible with the help of her friends. She knew that her own magic could not compete against the Alicorn Amulet, so Zecora taught her to use the power of friendship to pry the corrupting Alicorn Amulet away from Trixie. She apologizes for her behavior to a slightly skeptical Twilight.

FRIENDSHIP LESSON:

Zecora taught me so much about magic while I was in exile. She even taught me when not to use it. My magic alone wasn't powerful enough to take on the Alicorn Amulet head-to-head, so I needed to use a different kind of magic: the magic of friendship.

—Twilight Sparkle

EPISODE 306

Sleepless in Ponyville

After Rainbow Dash compliments Scootaloo on a scooter trick, Scootaloo desperately wants to become Rainbow Dash's protégé. She joins fellow Cutie Mark Crusaders Apple Bloom and Sweetie Belle, their big sisters, and Rainbow Dash on a camping trip just to get closer to her role model. On the trip, Rainbow Dash tells the group of ponies a scary story just before bedtime. It's the tale of the Headless Horse, haunting that very forest in search of her rusty old horseshoe. While Apple Bloom and Sweetie Belle turn to Applejack and Rarity for comfort, Scootaloo pretends that she isn't afraid in order to impress Rainbow Dash but spends the night terrified.

The next day, Scootaloo struggles to stay awake during their hike. When the ponies finally settle down for the evening, Rainbow Dash is back by the campfire continuing the Headless Horse tale to Scootaloo's dismay. Thoroughly afraid, she tries as hard as she can to postpone bedtime, but eventually everypony falls asleep. When Scootaloo falls asleep as well, she enters a horrible nightmare in which she is desperately trying to escape from the Headless Horse. The figure closes in on her and is then revealed to be Princess Luna.

In her dream, Princess Luna delivers a message to Scootaloo: She must face her real fear—not the Headless Horse, but the fear that Rainbow Dash will dislike her if she knows Scootaloo was scared. Scootaloo wakes up convinced she hears the Headless Horse outside the campsite and heads into the forest to track it down. Galloping around in the dark, she falls into a river, but Rainbow Dash comes to her rescue in the nick of time. Remembering Princess Luna's advice, Scootaloo confesses her true fear to Rainbow Dash and says she only ever wanted Rainbow Dash to take her under her wing. Rainbow Dash is touched by her honesty and literally takes the filly under her wing, granting Scootaloo's big wish.

FRIENDSHIP LESSON:

Everypony has fears, Scootaloo. Everypony must face them in their own way. But they must be faced. Or the nightmares will continue. Face your fears!
                    —Princess Luna

Wonderbolts Academy

R ainbow Dash is accepted to the Wonderbolts Academy in Cloudsdale and takes leave of Ponyville to start her training. When she arrives, she realizes that the training may be more than the trot in the park she imagined. She meets another Pegasus, Lightning Dust, who is able to match her in every imaginable feat of strength. The two become friends and are at the top of the pack.

The next day, the ponies are paired up. In each pair, there will be a lead pony and a wingpony. Their no-nonsense instructor, Spitfire, is certain that Lightning Dust and Rainbow Dash will make a great team, but Rainbow Dash is devastated to discover that she has been assigned to be the wingpony for Lightning Dust. The two Pegasi fly through their exercises together, consistently beating every other pony. Rainbow Dash isn't always comfortable with Lightning Dust's tactics—she often plays dirty in order to come out on top. But Rainbow Dash doesn't stop her because she wants to be seen as the very best, and at Wonderbolts Academy, that means being the toughest.

Meanwhile, in Ponyville, Pinkie Pie is anxiously awaiting a letter from Rainbow Dash. When it doesn't arrive, the ponies decide to take a trip to Cloudsdale in the hot air balloon. Unfortunately, just as they are arriving, Rainbow Dash and Lightning Dust create a tornado to "blow away" their competition. They lose control of the twister, and it heads straight for the Ponyville friends in their hot air balloon.

Rainbow Dash saves her friends from the tornado and becomes furious with Lightning Dust. She takes a stand against such dangerous flying, telling Spitfire that if recklessness is rewarded over responsibility at Wonderbolts Academy, she quits! Spitfire admires her courage, and instead of accepting her resignation, she tells Rainbow Dash that doing the right thing is an important part of being a Wonderbolt. Rainbow is promoted from wingpony to leader, while Lightning Dust is stripped of the title.

FRIENDSHIP LESSON:

Being the best should never come at the expense of our fellow ponies. It's not just about pushing ourselves; it's about pushing ourselves in the right direction.

—Spitfire

EPISODE 308

Apple Family Reunion

g ranny Smith is planning another Apple family reunion, and this
year *everypony* is coming. Applejack offers to take over the
planning so Granny can sit back, relax, and enjoy the event.
Granny agrees and brings out a photo album of past reunions. As she
fondly recalls the good times she's had with her family, Applejack takes
mental notes, wanting to make the reunion perfect.

The day of the reunion is here, and the entire Apple family has traveled
to Sweet Apple Acres from far and wide. Even Babs Seed has returned
from Manehattan! To their surprise, Applejack doles out fun, *fun*, FUN

tasks to everypony, determined to make this the most memorable reunion the Apples have ever had. She keeps them to a strict schedule, hustling each pony from one event to the next. Not only are the ponies annoyed that they don't have time to catch up with one another but the activities Applejack has planned are also grueling! Nopony is having much fun.

Applejack realizes that her determination to make this the best Apple reunion ever has resulted only in disaster. She apologizes to her family, and Granny Smith comforts her, reassuring her there is still plenty of time to make memories together before the reunion is over. Applejack gets an idea—one last activity for the whole family to do together. The Apple family participates in a barn raising, culminating in the traditional Apple family photo in front of the barn. The Apples spend the rest of the event catching up and enjoying one another's company. Applejack has learned that *who* you spend your time with is more important than *what* you spend that time doing.

FRIENDSHIP LESSON:

Dear Princess Celestia,

Today I learned a great lesson about family. Which, if you think about it, is really the first group of friends you ever make. Turns out that when you are with folks you care about, you don't have to do much to make that time memorable. Even the simplest of activities can take on a whole lot of meaning. And you'll find that you'll remember the "who" long after you've forgotten the "what."

Your humble Subject,
Applejack

Spike at Your Service

twilight Sparkle gives Spike the day off, and he decides to take a ride in the hot air balloon. But his clumsiness causes the balloon to float away before he boards. He chases it down, eventually finding himself in the middle of the Everfree Forest...and face-to-face with a pack of snarling timberwolves! Out of nowhere, Applejack comes to his rescue, allowing him to escape. Spike declares that Applejack has saved his life, and according to the Dragon Code, he must repay the debt by serving her for the rest of his days. He heads over to Golden Oak Library to break the news to Twilight, but she is too absorbed in her studies to process the gravity of Spike's message—that he will no longer be able to serve as her assistant.

Spike soon grows obsessed with helping Applejack. He refuses to accept that there is nothing she needs help with, but he is absolute in his adherence to the Dragon Code. Unfortunately for Applejack, Spike sometimes makes *more* rather than less work for Applejack. Applejack enlists the help of her friends to get Spike to understand she doesn't want him to live in her servitude forever. Twilight explains that there is only one way Spike will feel his debt is repaid—if he saves Applejack's life. Applejack confers with her friends and forms a plan: She will stage another timberwolf attack, but this time, *she* will be the victim.

The ponies fashion a timberwolf puppet, but Spike immediately recognizes it as a fake. Moments later, a real timberwolf comes bounding toward the gang. Applejack's hoof gets stuck between some rocks, and it isn't part of her act! Spike hangs back to help her. He throws a pebble into the timberwolf's mouth, causing him to choke and stop chasing the ponies. After Spike dislodges Applejack's hoof, she thanks him for saving her life. The two are glad that they are "even" and agree that, in the future, they will accept that friends help out friends, regardless of any type of honor code. Spike could not be happier to return to the library and Twilight's side.

FRiENDSHiP LESSON:

I know this code thing's important to you, but if somethin' like this comes up in the future, think maybe we can go back to my code—say "that's what friends do"—and leave it at that? I promise I won't think of you as any less noble.

—Applejack

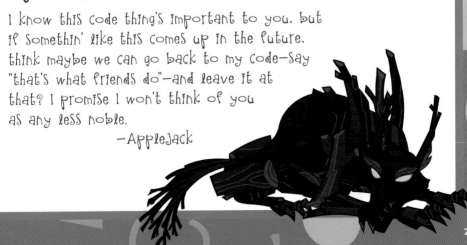

EPISODE 310

Keep Calm and Flutter on

Princess Celestia arrives in Ponyville with a most unusual task: find a way to help Discord change his mischievous, manipulative ways and persuade him to use his unique kind of magic for good instead of evil. She feels that Fluttershy has the special talents to reform him and assures the Ponyville friends that if Discord gets out of control, they can use the Elements of Harmony to turn him back into stone. When the ponies release Discord from his stony prison, he immediately starts creating mayhem and shatters the little confidence Fluttershy had. But the princess is counting on Fluttershy, and she is determined to succeed.

Fluttershy decides that the only way to reform Discord is to befriend him, and she invites him to make himself at home in her cottage. To nopony's surprise, he inflicts his own personal style on her home and soon it's in shambles. Twilight Sparkle, Rainbow Dash, Applejack, Rarity, and Pinkie Pie aren't convinced that kindness is the way to tame this Draconequus, but Fluttershy still insists that they are making great progress. To prove it, she invites the ponies over for a dinner party with Discord. He seems to be making an effort to behave, but everypony can sense mischief lurking behind his polite facade. Fluttershy's friends openly accuse Discord of lying about being reformed, and they are shocked when Fluttershy rushes to his defense. Discord appears genuinely touched when Fluttershy tells him to count her as a friend. A friend—his first and only friend!

Suddenly, Angel Bunny crashes the dinner party to report that Sweet Apple Acres has flooded. The girls are convinced that Discord has something to do with this.

At Sweet Apple Acres, Fluttershy implores Discord to return everything to its normal state. Amused, he flatly refuses, but it slowly dawns on him that if he does not make things right, he risks losing the trust of his only friend. Discord concedes, restoring Sweet Apple Acres. The ponies are amazed; could he truly be reformed? Princess Celestia returns, and Discord pledges to use his magic for good instead of evil. He's learned that friendship is something that is actually important to him. Fluttershy's friends are proud of her, and she is proud of Discord when he finally admits, "Friendship is magic."

FRIENDSHIP LESSON:

By treating Discord as a friend, [Fluttershy] got him to realize that friendship was actually important to him. And something that once he had, he didn't want to lose.

—Twilight Sparkle

Just for Sidekicks

g ems are Spike's favorite snack, and today he is attempting to bake
a delicious jewel cake, but he doesn't have enough gems! When
Fluttershy offers to pay Spike in jewels to pet-sit Angel Bunny,
Spike gets an idea. Spike offers to watch all the ponies' pets while
they are away—for a price. They all hand over their gems and head
off to the Crystal Empire. As soon as they leave, the pets are beyond
Spike's control.

Spike, seeing that there is no way he can pet-sit all these critters,
turns the pets over to the Cutie Mark Crusaders for the price of one of

his precious gems. But the fillies soon prove incapable of handling the responsibility, and Spike knows he has to take back the unruly pets. His charges are behaving worse than ever when Zecora offers Spike the solution to his pet problems for the price of another gem. Spike hands it over, but she simply donates it to charity and warns him of becoming too greedy. Spike really loses his cool this time as Granny Smith looks on. He gives Granny another gem to keep his secret. Spike continues to try wrangling the pets, but Angel Bunny is being particularly difficult, escaping onto the Friendship Express train. Spike, the Cutie Mark Crusaders, and all the pets board the train to retrieve Angel, but as soon as they board, the train leaves the station, bound for the Crystal Empire!

When they arrive at the Empire, Angel continues causing chaos, hopping off the train and darting in and out of the crowds. Spike is finally able to herd all the pets back onto the train, but his worries aren't over yet—his pony friends begin boarding the same train. Is Spike about to be caught by the very ponies who believe their precious pets are safe at home in Ponyville? As they hide, Spike apologizes to the pets for worrying more about the jewels than taking care of them. He delivers a special apology to Angel, who forgives him and cooperates in helping keep Spike's secret from the ponies.

FRIENDSHIP LESSON:

I wasn't really thinking about you at all—any of you.
Just wanted the jewels.
—Spike

EPISODE 312

games ponies Play

he Crystal Empire has been nominated to host the Equestria Games, the biggest sporting event in all of Equestria. The Empire is about to be visited by the games inspector, who will judge if it is the best place to host the games. Twilight Sparkle and her friends have been called up from Ponyville to join the welcome committee, ensuring that the Crystal Empire has the best possible chance of winning. Their mission is to greet Ms. Harshwhinny, the games inspector, at the train station and give her a perfect tour of the Empire before she meets with Princess Cadance. There's just one small snafu—Cadance's manestylist has fallen ill and there is nopony to create her traditional royal ceremonial headdress. But to Rarity, styling the mane of royalty sounds like the opportunity of a lifetime, so she steps up to the challenge.

Over at the Crystal Empire train station, Twilight, Applejack, Pinkie Pie, Fluttershy, and Rainbow Dash locate the pony who matches the description of Ms. Harshwhinny and welcome her with major fanfare. They take her on a grand tour of the castle and introduce her to Shining Armor. Ms. Harshwhinny is overly impressed with the Crystal Empire...much more than a worldly pony like herself should be. The girls are confused, until she reveals that she is just an ordinary tourist, not Ms. Harshwhinny at all. The girls panic when they realize that the *real* games inspector must be roaming around the Empire unwelcomed and unattended! Meanwhile, Rarity is having major challenges with Cadance's complicated manestyle, and they're all running out of time.

The ponies find the *real* Ms. Harshwhinny in the spa, voicing her complaints about the lack of a welcome reception to none other than the tourist pony who received the welcome committee's warm reception. The tourist describes to Ms. Harshwhinny all the wonderful experiences she had, and Ms. Harshwhinny is refreshed to hear an honest and unbiased opinion of a nominee for once. Once she finally meets Princess Cadance, whose hair is perfect now, her mind is made up. The Crystal Empire will be the next host of the Equestria Games!

FRIENDSHIP LESSON:

You know, it feels good to help others get something you always wanted but never had. Almost as good as getting it yourself. Almost.
—Rainbow Dash

EPISODE 313

Magical Mystery Cure

t wilight awakes one morning to find that her five best friends are sporting the wrong cutie marks—they've been switched! Twilight sees chaos all around Ponyville, from Rarity trying to control the weather to Pinkie Pie harvesting apples. Rainbow Dash is trying to care for the critters while Applejack is designing clothes. The previous night, Princess Celestia had asked Twilight to rewrite an ancient spell in one of her books. At first, Twilight believed the spell had no effect, but now she knows it accidentally switched her friends' cutie marks, causing them to do things they aren't good at.

Twilight reflects on how each of her friends has changed her life in their own unique ways. She then realizes that the only way she can fix this is through the magic of friendship. She gives each of her five friends tasks to help one another out that correspond with their *true* personalities. As they perform their tasks, the cutie marks return to their rightful owners and glow with the magic of friendship. When all five friends have been restored, a bright light shines from within Golden Oak Library. It is coming from the spellbook—the spell is rewriting itself! The light from the book engulfs Twilight Sparkle as she rises up into the air. When she reappears, she is sporting a pair of wings!

Princess Celestia appears and explains to Twilight that she has earned the wings through creating her own special magic—the magic of friendship. Everypony gathers in Canterlot to view Twilight Sparkle's coronation.

FRIENDSHIP LESSON:

We are gathered here today in celebration of a momentous occasion. My most faithful student, Twilight Sparkle, has done many extraordinary things since she's lived in Ponyville. She even helped reunite me with my sister, Princess Luna. But today, Twilight Sparkle did something extraordinary. She created new magic, proving without a doubt that she is ready to be crowned Equestria's newest princess! Fillies and gentlecolts, may I present for the very first time... Princess Twilight Sparkle!

—Princess Celestia

A little while ago, my teacher and mentor, Princess Celestia, sent me to live in Ponyville. She sent me to study friendship, which is something I didn't really care much about. But now, on a day like today, I can honestly say I wouldn't be standing here if it weren't for the friendships I've made with all of you.

Each one of you taught me something about friendship, and for that I will always be grateful. Today I consider myself the luckiest pony in Equestria. Thank you, friends! Thank you, everypony!

—Twilight Sparkle

"When
writing songs, I like
to start with the lyrics. The
rhythm of the spoken words usually
gives me ideas for the melody. Then, as
I get writing and have a theme, sometimes
I'll tweak and rework the lyrics to suit the
ideal musical phrases. I believe a great song
should be singable and playable in its most basic
form, so I like to start with just the tune and the
chords. It's like building the frame of a house
before putting in the walls, plumbing, and
decorations. I know that if the song sounds
good as a piano demo, it will sound great
when it's fully produced with all
the rest of the instruments."
—Daniel Ingram,
composer

THE MUSICAL PONY

Season 1

Song: "Laughter Song"
Episode: "Friendship is Magic, Part 2"
Lyrics by Lauren Faust
Music by Daniel Ingram

PINKIE PIE
Oh, girls, don't you see...?
When I was a little filly
and the sun was going down...
TWILIGHT SPARKLE
Tell me she's not...
PINKIE PIE
The darkness and the shadows,
they would always make me frown....
RARITY
She is.
PINKIE PIE
I'd hide under my pillow
from what I thought I saw,
but Grammy Pie said that wasn't the way
to deal with fears at all!
RAINBOW DASH
Then what is?
PINKIE PIE
She said, Pinkie, you gotta stand up tall.
Learn to face your fears.
You'll see that they can't hurt you;
just laugh to make them disappear!
Ha-ha-ha.
PONIES
[gasp]
PINKIE PIE
SOOOOOOOOOOOOOOOOOOOOOOOOO!

Giggle at the ghostly.
Guffaw at the grossly....
RAINBOW DASH
Guffaaaaww!!
PINKIE PIE
Crack up at the creepy....
RARITY
Ha-ha-ha-haaa!!!
PINKIE PIE
Whoop it up with the weepy....
APPLEJACK
Wooo-hoo-hooo!
PINKIE PIE
Chortle at the kooky....
TWILIGHT SPARKLE
K-k-hee-khee-khee!!
PINKIE PIE
Snortle at the spoooky....
PONIES
Aaaaahhh-ha-ha-ha!!
PINKIE PIE
Tell that big, dumb, scary face
to take a hike and leave you alone,
and if he thinks he can scare you,
then he's got another thing coming
and the very idea of such a thing
just makes you wanna—HAAAAAAAA-HA-
HA-HAAA-HA-HA-HA-HA-HA-HAAAAA-
HA-HAAAAAA-HA-HAAAAA—laugh!
PONIES
HA-HA-HA-HA-HA-HA-HA-HA!!!

Song: "Gala Fantasy Song"
Episode: "The Ticket Master"
Lyrics by Lauren Faust
Music by Daniel Ingram

PINKIE PIE
It's the most amazing-incredible-
tremendous-ginormous-super-fun-
wonderful-fabulous-terrifically
HUMONGOUS party in ALL OF
EQUESTRIA! I've *always, always,
ALWAYS* wanted to go!

Oh, the Grand Galloping Gala
is the best place for me.

Oh, the Grand Galloping Gala
is the best place for me.
Hip hip hooray, it's the best place for me,
for Pinkie!

With decorations, like streamers and fairy
lights and pinwheels and piñatas and
pincushions...

With goodies, like sugar cubes and
sugarcanes and sundaes and sunbeams
and sarsaparilla.

And I get to play my favoritest of favorite
fantabulous games, like Pin the Tail on the
Pony!

Oh, the Grand Galloping Gala
is the best place for me.

Oh, the Grand Galloping Gala
is the best place for me.

Cause it's the most galloprific, superly
terrific gala ever in the whole galaxy!
Whee!

Song: "Birthday Song"
Episode: "The Ticket Master"
Lyrics by Lauren Faust
Music by Daniel Ingram

PINKIE PIE AND PARTY
SURPRIIIIIISE!!!!!
PINKIE PIE
Twilight is my bestest friend,
whoopee, whoopee....
TWILIGHT SPARKLE
Pinkie...
PINKIE PIE
She's the cutest, smartest,
all-around best pony, pony....
TWILIGHT SPARKLE
Pinkie.
PINKIE PIE
I bet if I throw a super-duper fun
par-tee, par-tee...
TWILIGHT SPARKLE
Pinkie.
PINKIE PIE
She'll give her extra ticket to the Gala
to meeeeeeeeeee!

Song: "Winter Wrap Up Song"
Episode: "Winter Wrap Up"
Lyrics by Cindy Morrow
Music by Daniel Ingram

RAINBOW DASH
Three months of winter coolness
and awesome holidays.
PINKIE PIE
We've kept our hoofsies warm at home,
time off from work to plaaaaaay!
APPLEJACK
But the food we've stored is
runnin' out
and we can't grow in this cold.
RARITY
And even though I looove my boots
this fashion's getting old!
TWILIGHT SPARKLE
The time has come to welcome spring
and all things warm and green.
But it's also time to say good-bye.
It's winter. We must clean!
How can I help? I'm new, you see.
What does everypony do?
How do I fit in without magic?
I haven't got a clue!
CHORUS
Winter wrap-up! Winter wrap-up!
Let's finish our holiday cheer.
Winter wrap-up! Winter wrap-up!
'Cause tomorrow spring is here!
'Cause tomorrow spring is here!
RAINBOW DASH AND WEATHER TEAM
Bringing home the southern birds,
a Pegasus job begins,
and clearing all the gloomy skies
to let the sunshine in.

We move the clouds and
we melt the white snow.
When the sun comes up,
its warmth and beauty will glow.
CHORUS
Winter wrap-up! Winter wrap-up!
Let's finish our holiday cheer.
Winter wrap-up! Winter wrap-up!
'Cause tomorrow spring is here!
Winter wrap-up! Winter wrap-up!
'Cause tomorrow spring is here!
'Cause tomorrow spring is here!
FLUTTERSHY AND ANIMAL TEAM
Little critters hibernate
under the snow and ice.
We wake up all their sleepy heads,
so quietly and nice!
We help them gather up their food,
fix their homes below.
We welcome back the southern birds
so their families can grow!

CHORUS

Winter wrap-up! Winter wrap-up!
Let's finish our holiday cheer.
Winter wrap-up! Winter wrap-up!
'Cause tomorrow spring is here!
Winter wrap-up! Winter wrap-up!
'Cause tomorrow spring is here!
'Cause tomorrow spring is here!

APPLEJACK AND PLANT TEAM

No easy task to clear the ground,
plant our tiny seeds.
With proper care and sunshine,
everyone it feeds!
Apples, carrots, celery stalks,
colorful flowers, too.
We must work so very hard.
It's just so much to do!

CHORUS

Winter wrap-up! Winter wrap-up!
Let's finish our holiday cheer.
Winter wrap-up! Winter wrap-up!
'Cause tomorrow spring is here!
Winter wrap-up! Winter wrap-up!
'Cause tomorrow spring is here!
'Cause tomorrow spring is here!

TWILIGHT SPARKLE

Now that I know what they all do,
I have to find my place
and help with all of my heart.

Tough task ahead I face!
How will I do without my magic?
Help the Earth pony way?
I want to belong, so I must
do my best today!
Do my best today!

CHORUS

Winter wrap-up! Winter wrap-up!
Let's finish our holiday cheer.
Winter wrap-up! Winter wrap-up!
'Cause tomorrow spring is here!
Winter wrap-up! Winter wrap-up!

TWILIGHT SPARKLE

'Cause tomorrow spring is here!
'Cause tomorrow spring is here!
'Cause tomorrow spring is here!

Song: "Cupcake Song"
Episode: "Call of the Cutie"
Lyrics by Meghan McCarthy
Music by Daniel Ingram

PINKIE PIE

All you have to do is take a cup of flour.
Add it to the mix.
Now just take a little something sweet,
not sour.
A bit of salt, just a pinch.
Baking these treats is such a cinch.
Add a teaspoon of vanilla.
Add a little more and you count to four,
and you'll never get your fill-a....
Cupcakes! So sweet and tasty! Cupcakes!
Don't be too hasty! Cupcakes! Cupcakes!
Cupcakes! Cupcaaaakes!

Song: "Stitching It Together"
Episode: "Suited for Success"
Lyrics by Charlotte Fullerton
Music by Daniel Ingram

RARITY
Thread by thread,
stitching it together,
Twilight's dress.
Cutting out the pattern, snip by snip,
making sure the fabric falls nicely,
it's the perfect color and so hip.
Always got to keep in mind my pacing,
making sure the clothes correctly facing
I'm stitching Twilight's dress....

Yard by yard, fussing on the details.
Jeweled neckline?
Don't you know a stitch in time saves nine?
Make her something perfect to inspire
even though she hates formal attire.
Got to mind those intimate details
even though she's more concerned
with sales.
It's Applejack's new dress.

Dressmaking's easy.
For Pinkie Pie, something pink.
Fluttershy, something breezy.
Blend color and form—
do you think it looks cheesy?

Something brash, perhaps quite fetching?
Hook and eye,
couldn't you just simply die?
Making sure it fits forelock and crest.
Don't forget some magic in the dress.
Even though it rides high on the flank,

Rainbow won't look like a tank.
I'm stitching Rainbow's dress.

Piece by piece,
snip by snip,
croup, dock, haunch,
shoulders, hip.
Thread by thread,
primmed and pressed,
yard by yard,
never stressed.
And that's the art of the dressssssss!

RARITY
Stitch by stitch,
stitching it together.
Deadline looms.
Don't you know the client's always right,
even if my fabric choice was perfect.
Got to get them all done by tonight.
Pinkie Pie, that color's too obtrusive,
wait until you see it in the light.
I'm sewing them together.

Hour by hour,
one more change,
I'm sewing them together.
Take great pains.
Fluttershy, you're putting me in a bind.
Rainbow Dash, what is on your mind?
Oh my gosh, there's simply not much time.
Don't forget Applejack's duds must
shiiiiiine.

Dressmaking's easy.
Every customer's call
brings a whole new revision.
Have to pick up the pace,
still hold to my vision.
PINKIE PIE
All we ever want is indecision.
RAINBOW DASH
All we really like is what we know.
TWILIGHT SPARKLE
Got to balance style with adherence.
FLUTTERSHY
Making sure we make a good appearance.
APPLEJACK
Even if you simply have to fudge it.

**PINKIE PIE, RAINBOW DASH,
TWILIGHT SPARKLE, FLUTTERSHY,
AND APPLEJACK**
Make sure that it stays within our budget!
RARITY
Got to overcome intimidation.
Remember, it's all in the presentation!
Piece by piece,
snip by snip,
croup, dock, haunch,
shoulders, hip.
Bolt by bolt,
primmed and pressed,
yard by yard,
always stressed.
And that's the art of the dressssssss!

Song: "Hush Now, Quiet Now"
Episode: "Stare Master"
Lyrics by Chris Savino
Music by Daniel Ingram

FLUTTERSHY
How about I sing you a lullaby?
ALL THREE GIRLS
Yeah!
FLUTTERSHY
Ahem...
Hush now, quiet now,
it's time to lay your sleepy head.
Hush now, quiet now,
it's time to go to bed.
SWEETIE BELLE
I know this one!!!
FLUTTERSHY
Oh, how wonderful!
Why don't you sing it with me?

SWEETIE BELLE
Ahem...
Hush now, quiet now,
time to lay your sleepy head.
Said, hush now, quiet now,
it's time to go to beeeeeeed.
FLUTTERSHY
Okay, Sweetie, that was—
SWEETIE BELLE
Drifting off to sleep,
the exciting day's behind you.
Drifting off to sleep,
let the joy of dreamland find you.
FLUTTERSHY
Thank you, Sweetie, I'm—
SWEETIE BELLE
Hush now, quiet now,
lay your sleepy head.
Said, hush now, quiet now,
it's time to go to BEEEEEEEEEEEEEEEEE-
EEEEEEEEEEEEEEEEEEEEEEED!!!!!

Song: "Cutie Mark Crusaders Song"
Episode: "The Show Stoppers"
Lyrics by Cindy Morrow
Music by Daniel Ingram

SCOOTALOO
Look! Here are three little ponies
ready to sing for this crowd.
Listen up, cause here's our story.
I'm gonna sing it—
**APPLE BLOOM, SWEETIE BELLE, AND
SCOOTALOO**
VERY LOUD!

SCOOTALOO
When you're a younger pony
and your flank is very bare.
Feels like the sun will never come
when your cutie mark's not there.
So the three of us, we fight the fight.
There is nothing that we fear.
We'll have to figure out what we'll do next—
**APPLE BLOOM, SWEETIE BELLE, AND
SCOOTALOO**
'til our cutie marks are here!
We are the Cutie Mark Crusaders
on a quest to find out who we are
and we will never stop the journey,
not until we have our cutie marks.
SCOOTALOO
They all say that you'll get your mark
when the time is really right
and you know just what
you're s'posed to do
and your talent comes to light.
But it's not as easy as it sounds
and that waiting's hard to do.
So we test our talents everywhere—
**APPLE BLOOM, SWEETIE BELLE, AND
SCOOTALOO**
until our face is blue!
We are the Cutie Mark Crusaders
on a quest to find out who we are
and we will never stop the journey,
not until we have our cutie marks.
We are the Cutie Mark Crusaders
on a quest to find out who we are
and we will never stop the journey,
not until we have our cutie maaaaarks!

Song: "Sharing/Caring Song"
Episode: "Over a Barrel"
Lyrics by Amy Keating Rogers
Music by Daniel Ingram

PINKIE PIE
We may be divided,
but of you all I beg
to remember we're all hooved
at the end of each leg.

No matter what the issue,
come from wherever you please,
all this fighting gets you nothing
but hoof-and-mouth disease.

Arguing's not the way.
Hey, come out and play.
It's a shiny new day.
So whaddaya say?

You gotta shaaaaaare.
You gotta caaaaaare.
It's the right thing to do.
You gotta shaaaaaare.
You gotta caaaaaare.
And there'll always be a way through.

Both our diets, I should mention,
are completely vegetarian.
We all eat hay and oats.
Why be at each other's throat?

You gotta shaaaaaare.
You gotta caaaaaare.
It's the right thing to do.
Aand there'll always be a way—
throoooooooough!

Song: "Fluttershy Fantasy Song"
Episode: "The Cutie Mark Chronicles"
Lyrics by Mitch Larson
Music by Daniel Ingram

YOUNG FLUTTERSHY
What is this place
filled with so many wonders?
Casting its spell
that I am now under.
Squirrels in the trees
and the cute little bunnies.
Birds flying free
and bees with their honey,
hooooneeeeeey!
Ooooooh!
What a magical place!
And I owe it all
to the Pegasus race!
If I knew the ground had
so much up its sleeve,
I'd have come here sooner
and never leave.
Yes, I
love
ev—ry—THIIIIIIIIING!!

Song: "Singing Telegram Song"
Episode: "Party of One"
Lyrics by Meghan McCarthy
Music by Daniel Ingram

PINKIE PIE
This is your singing telegram.
I hope it finds you well.
You're invited to a party
'cause we think you're really swell.
Gummy's turning one year old,
so help us celebrate.
The cake will be delicious,
the festivities first-rate.
There will be games and dancing.
Bob for apples, cut a rug.
And when the party's over,
we'll gather around for a group hug.
No need to bring a gift.
Being there will be enough.
Birthdays mean having fun with friends,
not getting lots of stuff.
It won't be the same without you,
so we hope that you say yes.
So, please, oh, please RSVP,
and come and be our guest.

Song: "At the Gala"
Episode: "The Best Night Ever"
Lyrics by Amy Keating Rogers
Music by Daniel Ingram

TWILIGHT SPARKLE
At the Gala!
PONY FRIENDS
At the Gala!

FLUTTERSHY
At the Gala, in the Garden,
I am going to see them all.
All the creatures, I'll befriend them...
at the Gala.
PONY FRIENDS
At the Gala!
FLUTTERSHY
All the birdies and the critters,
they will love me, big and small.
We'll become good friends forever
right here at the Gala!
PONY FRIENDS
All our dreams will come true
right here at the Gala!
At the Gala!
APPLEJACK
At the Gala, I will sell them
all my apple-tastic treats!
Hungry ponies...
they will buy them.
Caramel apples, apple sweets!

"In the first draft of 'The Cutie Pox,' Sweetie Belle and Scootaloo sang a rap to Apple Bloom, hoping to cheer her up. That got cut very early on. In 'The Best Night Ever,' I had Fluttershy singing to Celestia's animals to try to get them to come out. That script ran really long, so that was cut, too."
—Amy Keating Rogers, writer

PONY FRIENDS
It's amazing!
Better hurry!
Yummy yum!
Feeling snacky!
Bring your money!
Gimme some!
APPLEJACK
And I'll earn a lot of money
for the Apple family!
PONY FRIENDS
All our dreams and our hopes
from now until hereafter.
All that we've been wishing for
will happen at the Gala!
At the Gala!
RARITY
At the Gala, all the royals,
they will meet fair Rarity.
They will see I'm just as regal
at the Gala!
PONY FRIENDS
At the Gala!

RARITY
I will find him,
my Prince Charming.
And how gallant he will be...
he will treat me like a lady...
tonight at the Gala!
PONY FRIENDS
This is what we've waited for,
to have the Best Night Ever!
Each of us will live our dreams
tonight at the Gala!
At the Gala!
RAINBOW DASH
I've been dreaming.
I've been waiting
to fly with those great ponies...
the Wonderbolts!
Their daring tricks,
spinning round and having kicks!
Perform for crowds of thousands!
They'll shower us with diamonds!
The Wonderbolts will see me
right here at the Gala!

PONY FRIENDS
All we've longed for,
all we've dreamed...
our happy ever after.
Finally will all come true
right here at the Grand Gala!
At the Gala!

PINKIE PIE
I am here at the Grand Gala!
For it is the best party!
But the one thing it was missing
was a pony named Pinkie!
For I am the best at parties!
All the ponies will agree!
Ponies playing, ponies dancing
with me at the Grand Gala!

PONY FRIENDS
Happiness and laughter at the Gala!
At the Gala!

TWILIGHT SPARKLE
At the Gala...with the princess
is where I am going to be.
We will talk all about magic
and of what I've learned and seen.
It is going to be so special
as she takes time just for me!

PONY FRIENDS
This will be the Best Night Ever!
Into the Gala we must go...
we're ready now, we're all aglow.
Into the Gala, let's go in
and have the Best Night Ever.
Into the Gala, now's the time.
We're ready and we look divine.

FLUTTERSHY
Into the Gala to meet new friends!

APPLEJACK
Into the Gala to sell some apples!

RARITY
Into the Gala to find my prince!

RAINBOW DASH
To prove I'm great, as a Wonderbolt is!

FLUTTERSHY
To meet...

APPLEJACK
To sell...

RARITY
To find...

RAINBOW DASH
To prove...

PINKIE PIE
To whoop...

TWILIGHT SPARKLE
To talk...

PONY FRIENDS
Into the Gala...
into the Gala...
and we'll have the Best Night Ever!
At the Gala!

Song: "Pony Pokey"
Episode: "The Best Night Ever"
Lyrics by Amy Keating Rogers
Music by Daniel Ingram

PINKIE PIE
You reach your right hoof in,
you reach your right hoof out.
You reach your right hoof in,
and you shake it all about.
You do the Pony Pokey,
meeting lots of folks with clout.
That's what I'm talking about!

You step your left hoof in,
you pull it right back out.

You step your left hoof in,
but you better help him out.
You do the Pony Pokey,
but you find a different crowd.
That's what it's all about!

You kick your back left in,
you pull your back left out.
You reach your back left in,
just be brave and have no doubt.
You do the Pony Pokey,
feeling like you're gonna pout.
That's what I'm singing about!

You tilt your head in,
you tilt your head out.
You tilt your head in,
then you shake it all about.
You do the Pony Pokey,
even though your date's a lout.
You're better off without!

You stomp your whole self in,
you stomp your whole self out.
You stomp your whole self in,
and you stomp yourself about.
You do the Pony Pokey,
and you give a little shout.

FLUTTERSHY
COME OUT!

PINKIE PIE
That's what I'm talking about!
You do the Pony Pokey!
You do the Pony Pokey!
You do the Pony Pokey!
And that's what it's all about.
Yeah!

Song: "Jolly Good Fellow"
Episode: "The Best Night Ever"
Lyrics by Amy Keating Rogers
Music by Daniel Ingram

PINKIE PIE
I'm at the Grand Galloping Gala!
I'm at the Grand Galloping Gala!
I'm at the Grand Galloping Gala!
It's all I ever dreamed!
It's all I ever dreamed!
Woo hoo!
It's all I ever dreamed!
Yippee!
I'm at the Grand Galloping Galaaaaaa!
It's all I've ever dreamed!

"Songs work really well
in *My Little Pony: Friendship is
Magic* for different reasons, but they are
all motivated by the characters. I think this is
why it works so well when the show has songs.
The songs can also make the stakes of the
episode that much bigger, and when things
don't go right, the impact is greater."
—Amy Keating Rogers, writer

Season 2

Song: "May the Best Pet Win"
Episode: "May the Best Pet Win!"
Lyrics by Charlotte Fullerton & Kevin Rubio
Music by Daniel Ingram

FLUTTERSHY
Now, Rainbow, my dear,
I cannot express my delight.
It's abundantly clear
that somewhere out here
is the pet that will suit you just right.

RAINBOW DASH
I can't wait to get started,
but first let me set a few rules.
It's of utmost importance
the pet that I get is something
that's awesome and cool!

FLUTTERSHY
Awesome. Cool. Got it.
I have so many wonderful choices.
Just wait, you will see.

RAINBOW DASH
I need something real fast like a bullet
to keep up with me.

FLUTTERSHY
Sure. How 'bout a bunny?
They're cutesy and wootsy
and quick as can be.

RAINBOW DASH
Cutesy? Wootsy?
Have you even met me?

FLUTTERSHY
Rainbow, have faith.
You see, I will bet you

somewhere in here is
a pet that will get you.
Come on, the sky's the limit!

RAINBOW DASH
Sky is good! I'd like it to fly.

FLUTTERSHY
Really? Because I think this
widdle puddy tat has your name
written all over it. Yes, he does.
Aw, look. He likes you!

RAINBOW DASH
Pass.

FLUTTERSHY
I have so many wonderful choices
for you to decide!
There are otters and seals
with massive appeal.

RAINBOW DASH
Otters and seals do not fly.

FLUTTERSHY
Maybe not, but I've seen
this particular seal catch ten feet of air
when he breaches the water.

RAINBOW DASH
That's it. I'm outta here.

FLUTTERSHY
Wait! There must be a pet here
that will fit the ticket.
How about a ladybug?
Or a cute cricket?

RAINBOW DASH
Bigger. And. Cooler.

FLUTTERSHY
Bigger. Cooler. Right.

228

I've got just the thing
in that tree!
Dash, meet your new fabulous pet,
Squirrely!

RAINBOW DASH

It's just a squirrel.

FLUTTERSHY

Not just any squirrel...
a flying squirrel!

RAINBOW DASH

Yeahhhh, so like I was saying—
Fluttershy, pal,
this won't cut it.
I need a pet to keep up with me.
Something awesome!
Something flying!
With coolness that defies gravity!

FLUTTERSHY

I'm sensing you want
an animal that can fly.

RAINBOW DASH

Ya think??

FLUTTERSHY

I have plenty of wonderful
creatures who soar in the sky.
Like a sweet hummingbird
or a giant monarch butterfly?

RAINBOW DASH

Better. But cooler!

FLUTTERSHY

I see.
How 'bout an owl?
Or a wasp or a toucan?
There's so many wonderful creatures
the likes of that.
There are falcons and eagles,
they are both quite regal.
Or perhaps what you need
is a dark and mysterious bat?

RAINBOW DASH

Now you're talking!
But instead of just one standout,
now that's too many!
So many choices,
and such riches aplenty!

FLUTTERSHY

Not a bad problem to have,
if you ask me.

RAINBOW DASH

The bat would be awesome!
But the wasp I'm digging, too.
Do you have something
in a yellow-striped bat?

FLUTTERSHY

No. But I've got a hot-pink
flamingo just dying to meet you.

RAINBOW DASH

What to do, what to do?
A prize? That's it!
There's really just one way
to find out which animal's best.
Hold a contest of speed, agility, and guts
that will put each pet to the test!

FLUTTERSHY

Don't forget style.
That should be considered.

RAINBOW DASH

Then I'll know for sure
who's best of the litter!

FLUTTERSHY

The one who is awesome-est, cool.

RAINBOW DASH
Just like me!
Can't settle for less
'cause I'm the best!
RAINBOW DASH AND FLUTTERSHY
So a contest we will seeeeeeee...
RAINBOW DASH
who's the number one, greatest,
perfect-est pet in the world for me!
RAINBOW DASH AND FLUTTERSHY
May the games begin!
RAINBOW DASH
And may the best pet win.

Song: "Becoming Popular
(The Pony Everypony Should Know)"
Episode: "Sweet and Elite"
Lyrics by Meghan McCarthy
Music by Daniel Ingram

RARITY
I'll be the toast of the town,
the girl on the go.
I'm the type of pony everypony,
everypony should know....
I'll be the one to watch,
the girl in the flow.
I'm the type of pony everypony,
everypony should know....

Becoming as popular as popular can be.
Making my mark, making my mark
in high society.
I'm the belle of the ball,
the star of the show.
Yeah, I'm the type of pony everypony,
everypony should know.

See how they hang on every word
that I speak.
My approving glance is what they all seek.
I'm the crème de la crème,
not just another Jane Doe.
I'm the type of pony everypony,
everypony should know.

At home, at the opera, on a fancy yacht
becoming the talk,
the talk of all of Canterlot.
I'm the crème de la crème,
not just another Jane Doe.
Yeah, I'm the type of pony everypony,
everypony should know.

Because...I'm the type of pony,
yes, I'm the type of pony,
yes, I'm the type of pony
everypony should know....

Song: "Heart Carol Song" or
"A Circle of Friends"
Episode: "Hearth's Warming Eve"
Lyrics by Merriwether Williams
Music by Daniel Ingram

EVERYPONY
The Fire of Friendship lives in our hearts.
As long as it burns we cannot drift apart.
Though quarrels arise,
their numbers are few.
Laughter and singing will see us through.
We are a circle of pony friends...
a circle of friends we'll be
to the very end.

Song: "Baby Cakes Song"
Episode: "Baby Cakes"
Lyrics by Charlotte Fullerton
Music by Daniel Ingram

PINKIE PIE
Happy month-i-versary
to you and you today!
I-can't-believe-you're-already-a-month-
old. Time-sure-flies-doesn't-it-wow.
Seems-like-only-yesterday-
you-were-born.
But now you're a month old today, hey!

Song: "Piggy Song"
Episode: "Baby Cakes"
Lyrics by Amy Keating Rogers
Music by Daniel Ingram

PINKIE PIE
First you jiggle your tail,
oink, oink, oink!
Then you wriggle your snout,
oink, oink, oink!
Then you wriggle your rump,
oink, oink, oink!
Then shout it out!
Oink, oink, oink!
[Repeat]
First jiggle your tail,
oink, oink, oink!
Then you wriggle your snout,
oink, oink, oink!
Then you wriggle your rump,
oink, oink, oink!
Then shout it out!
Oink, oink, oink!

[Repeat faster]
First jiggle your tail,
oink, oink, oink!
Then you wriggle your snout,
oink, oink, oink!
Then you wriggle your rump,
oink, oink, oink!
Then shout it out!
Oink, oink, oink!

Song: "Flim Flam Cider Song"
Episode: "The Super Speedy Cider
Squeezy 6000"
Lyrics by Mitch Larson & Daniel Ingram
Music by Daniel Ingram

FLIM
Well, lookie what we got here,
brother of mine.
It's the same in every town.
Ponies with thirsty throats, dry tongues,
and not a drop of cider to be found.
Maybe they're not aware that there's
really no need for this teary despair.
FLAM
That the key that they need to solve this
sad cider shortage you and I will share.
FLIM AND FLAM
Well, you got opportunity
in this very community!
He's Flim—
he's Flam. We're the world-famous
Flim Flam brothers, traveling salesponies
nonpareil!
PINKIE PIE
Nonpa-what?

231

FLIM

Nonpareil! And that's exactly
the reason why, you see—
Nopony else in this whole place
will give you such a chance to be where
you need to be.
And that's a new world with tons of cider,
fresh-squeezed and ready for drinking.

FLAM

More cider than you could drink in all
your days of thinking!

RAINBOW DASH

I doubt that—

FLIM AND FLAM

So take this opportunity in this very
community!

FLAM

He's Flim—

FLIM

he's Flam. We're the world-famous
Flim Flam brothers, traveling salesponies
nonpareil!

FLIM

I suppose by now you're wondering
about our peculiar mode of transport.

FLAM

I say, our mode of locomotion.

FLIM

And I suppose by now you're wondering,
where is this promised cider?

FLAM

Anyhorse can make a claim
and anypony can do the same.

FLIM

But my brother and I have something
most unique and superb,
unseen at any time in this big, new world.

FLIM AND FLAM

And that's opportunity!

FLIM

Folks, it's the one and only—
the biggest and the best—

FLAM

the unbelievable—

FLIM

unimpeachable—

FLAM

indispensable—

FLIM

I-can't-believe-able—

FLIM AND FLAM

Flim Flam brothers Super Speedy
Cider Squeezy 6ooo!

"I have a soft spot for the
Flim Flam brothers' song. It was just so
much fun to write—both because of its unique patter-
like quality and because of what the brothers are trying
to accomplish with the song: They want to mesmerize
Ponyville. And it's catchy as heck."
—Mitch Larson, writer

FLAM
Whattaya say, sister?
PONIES
Oh, we got opportunity
in this very community!
Please, Flim, please, Flam,
help us outta this jam
with your Flim Flam brothers
Super Speedy Cider Squeezy 6000!
FLIM
Young filly, I would be ever so honored if
you might see fit to let my brother
and I borrow some of your delicious—
and might I add spellbindingly fragrant—
apples for our little demonstration here?
APPLEJACK
Uh...sure, I guess.
PONIES
Opportunity!
In our community!
FLAM
Ready, Flim?
FLIM
Ready, Flam!
FLAM
Let's bing, bang, zam
and show these thirsty ponies
a world of delectable cider!
PONIES
Cider...cider...cider...cider...
cider...cider...cider...cider...
FLIM
Watch closely, my friends—
FLAM
the fun begins!
FLIM
Now here's where the magic happens,

right here, in this heaving,
roiling cider press coiling
guts of the very machine.
Those apples plucked fresh
are right now as we speak
being turned into grade A, top-notch,
five-star, blow-your-horseshoes-off,
one-of-a-kind cider.
FLIM
Feel free to take a sneak peek.
GRANNY SMITH
Now wait, you fellers, hold it!
You went and oversold it.
I guarantee that what you have there
won't compare,
for the very most important ingredient
can't be added or done expedient,
and that's quality, friends,
Apple Acres' quality and care!
FLIM
Well, Granny, I'm glad you brought that
up, my dear.
I say, I'm glad you brought that up.
You see that we are very picky when it
comes to cider, if you'll kindly try a cup....
FLAM
Yes, sir, yes, ma'am, this great machine
lets just the very best....
So whattaya say, then, Apples?
Care to step into the modern world and
put the Super Speedy Cider Squeezy 6000
to the test?
PONIES
Cider...cider...cider...cider...
FLIM
Whattaya think, folks?
Do you see what the Apples can't?

I see it clear as day! I know she does!
So does he! Come on, Ponyville,
you know what I'm talking about!

FLIM AND FLAM
We're saying you've got opportunity
in this very community!
He's Flim, he's Flam.
We're the world-famous
Flim Flam brothers...
tra-vel-ing saaaalesponies
NONPAREIIIIIIIL!!
Yeeeeaaaaahh!!

Song: "The Perfect Stallion"
Episode: "Hearts and Hooves Day"
Lyrics by Meghan McCarthy
Music by Daniel Ingram

SWEETIE BELLE
Cheerilee is sweet and kind.
She's the best teacher we could hope for.
The perfect stallion you and I must find,
one to really make her heart soar.
But this one's too young,
this one's too old—
he clearly has a terrible cold.

SICKLY PONY
Aah-choo.

APPLE BLOOM
This guy's too silly.
He's way too uptight.

UPPITY PONY
I say!

SWEETIE BELLE
Well, nothing's wrong with this one.
He seems all right.

SCOOTALOO
His girlfriend sure thinks so.

SWEETIE BELLE
How 'bout this one?

APPLE BLOOM
He's much too flashy.

SCOOTALOO
He might do.

APPLE BLOOM AND SWEETIE BELLE
If he weren't so splashy.

APPLE BLOOM
Too short.

SWEETIE BELLE
Too tall.

APPLE BLOOM
Too clean.

SCOOTALOO
Too smelly.

SWEETIE BELLE
Too strangely obsessed with tubs of jelly.

APPLE BLOOM
I don't think that we're mistaken.
It seems all the good ones are taken.

SWEETIE BELLE
I really feel that at this rate,
we'll never find the perfect date.
Don't want to quit and give up hope...

SCOOTALOO
Doing anything special for
Hearts and Hooves Day?

SWEETIE BELLE
Oh please, oh please, oh please say...

BIG MCINTOSH
nope.

SWEETIE BELLE
We did it, girls, we've found the one
who will send our teacher's heart aflutter.

Song: "The Smile Song"
Episode: "A Friend in Deed"
Lyrics by Amy Keating Rogers
Music by Daniel Ingram

PINKIE PIE

My name is Pinkie Pie!
Hello!
And I am here to say
how ya doin'?
I'm gonna make you smile and I will
brighten up your day!
It doesn't matter now.
What's up?
If you are sad or blue.
Howdy!
'Cause cheering up my friends is just
what Pinkie's here to do!

'Cause I love to make you smile, smile,
smile. Yes, I do.
It fills my heart with sunshine all the
while. Yes, it does.
'Cause all I really need's a
smile, smile, smile.
From these happy friends of mine!

I like to see you grin.
Awesome!

I love to see you beam.
Rock on!
The corners of your mouth turned up is
always Pinkie's dream.
Hoof bump!
But if you're kinda worried—
and your face has made a frown—
I'll work real hard and do my best
to turn that sad frown upside down!

'Cause I love to make you grin, grin, grin.
Yes, I do.
Bust it out from ear to ear. Let it begin.
Just give me a joyful grin, grin, grin.
And you fill me with good cheer!

It's true, some days are dark and lonely.
And maybe you feel sad.
But Pinkie will be there to show you
that it isn't that bad.
There's one thing that makes me happy
and makes my whole life worthwhile.
And that's when I talk to my friends and
get them to smi-i-ile!

I really am so happy!
Your smile fills me with glee.
I give a smile, I get a smile,
and that's so special to me.

"I would probably say that
'The Smile Song' is my favorite because it's
just so uplifting and positive without being too
saccharine or cheesy. It strikes a great balance of
fun and meaning. There's no way you can listen to
that and not feel better for doing so."
—Jayson Thiessen, supervising director

'Cause I love to see you
beam, beam, beam. Yes, I do.
Tell me, what more can I say
to make you see that I do?
It makes me happy when you
beam, beam, beam.
Yes, it always makes my day!

Come on, everypony, smile, smile, smile.
Fill my heart up with sunshine, sunshine.
All I really need's a smile, smile, smile,
from these happy friends of mine!

Come on, everypony, smile, smile, smile,
fill my heart up with sunshine, sunshine.
All I really need's a smile, smile, smile,
from these happy friends of mine!
Yes, the perfect gift for me-ee-ee
is a smile as wide as a mi-ii-ile.
To make me happy as can be-ee-ee.

PINKIE PIE AND FRIENDS

Smile! Smile! Smile! Smile! Smiiiiiiiiiile!
Come on and smile! Come on and smile!

Song: "The Cranky Doodle Song, Part 1"
Episode: "A Friend in Deed"
Lyrics by Amy Keating Rogers
Music by Daniel Ingram

PINKIE PIE

You're a Cranky Doodle Donkey guy!
A Cranky Doodle Donkey!
I've never met you,
but you're my new friend.
And I'm your best friend, Pinkie Pie!
C'mon now, Doodle, give a smile!!!!

Song: "The Cranky Doodle Song, Part 2"
Episode: "A Friend in Deed"
Lyrics by Amy Keating Rogers
Music by Daniel Ingram

PINKIE PIE

He had a Cranky Doodle sweetheart,
she's his Cranky Doodle joy.
I helped the Cranky Doodle boy.
Yes, I helped the Cranky Doodle boy!!

Song: "Welcome Ditty"
Episode: "A Friend in Deed"
Lyrics by Amy Keating Rogers
Music by Daniel Ingram

PINKIE PIE

Welcome, welcome, welcome!
A fine welcome to you!
Welcome, welcome, welcome!
I say, "How do you do?"
Welcome, welcome, welcome!
I say, "Hip hip hooray!"
Welcome, welcome, welcome
to Ponyville todaaaaaaaaay!

Song: "BBBFF"
Episode: "A Canterlot Wedding, Part 1"
Lyrics by Meghan McCarthy
Music by Daniel Ingram

TWILIGHT SPARKLE

When I was just a filly,
I found it rather silly
to see how many other ponies
I could meet....
I had my books to read.
Didn't know that I would ever need
other ponies to make my life complete.
But there was one colt that I cared for.
I knew he would be there for...me.
My Big Brother Best Friend Forever.
Like two peas in a pod,
we did everything together.
He taught me how to fly a kite.
Best friend forever.
We never had a single fight.
We did everything together.
We shared our hopes.

> "'BBBFF'
> is special to me
> because as I was writing
> the lyrics I was thinking
> about the amazing relationship
> that my daughter has with her
> big brother. If they start to get on
> each other's nerves as they get
> older, I'm going to force them
> to listen to it on a loop until
> they make up."
> —Meghan McCarthy,
> story editor

We shared our dreams.
I miss him more than I realized,
it seems....

PONIES

Your Big Brother Best Friend Forever.
Like two peas in a pod,
you did everything together.

TWILIGHT SPARKLE

And though he's oh-so-far away.
I hoped that he would stay...
my Big Brother Best Friend Forever.
Forever.

Song: "This Day Aria, Part 1"
Episode: "A Canterlot Wedding, Part 2"
Lyrics by Meghan McCarthy
Music by Daniel Ingram

IMPOSTOR CADANCE

This day is going to be perfect.
The kind of day of which I've dreamed
since I was small.
Everypony will gather round,
say I look lovely in my gown.
What they don't know is that
I have fooled them all.

PRINCESS CADANCE

This day was going to be perfect.
The kind of day of which I've dreamed
since I was small.
But instead of having cake
with all my friends to celebrate,
my wedding bells, they may not ring
for me at all.

IMPOSTOR CADANCE

I could care less about the dress.
I won't partake in any cake.

Vows? Well, I'll be lying when I say
that through any kind of weather
I'll want us to be together.
The truth is I don't care for him at all.
No, I do not love the groom.
In my heart there is no room.
But I still want him to be all mine!

PRINCESS CADANCE

Must escape before it's too late.
Find a way to save the day.
Hope? I'll be lying if I say
I don't fear that I may lose him
to one who wants to use him,
not care for, love, and cherish him
each day.
For I oh-so-love the groom.
All my thoughts he does consume.
Oh, Shining Armor, I'll be there very
soooooooon!

IMPOSTOR CADANCE

Finally the moment has arrived
for me to be one lucky bride....

PRINCESS CADANCE

Oh, the wedding we won't make.
He'll end up marrying a fake.
Shining Armor will be—

IMPOSTOR CADANCE

Mine, all mine.

Song: "This Day Aria, Part 2"
Episode: "A Canterlot Wedding, Part 2"
Lyrics by Meghan McCarthy
Music by Daniel Ingram

QUEEN CHRYSALIS

This day has been just perfect.

The kind of day of which I've dreamed
since I was small.
Everypony I'll soon control,
every stallion, mare, and foal.
Who says a girl can't really have it all?

Song: "Love Is in Bloom"
Episode: "A Canterlot Wedding, Part 2"
Lyrics by Meghan McCarthy &
Daniel Ingram
Music by Daniel Ingram

TWILIGHT SPARKLE

Love is in bloom.
A beautiful bride. A handsome groom.
Two hearts becoming one.
A bond that cannot be undone because
love is in bloom.
A beautiful bride. A handsome groom.
I say, love is in bloom.
You're starting a life
and making room for us.

Season 3

Song: "The Failure Song"
Episode: "The Crystal Empire, Part 1"
Lyrics by Meghan McCarthy
Music by Daniel Ingram

TWILIGHT SPARKLE
I was prepared to do my best,
thought I could handle any test,
for I can do so many tricks,
but I wasn't prepared for this.
Levitation would have been a breeze.
Facts and figures I recite with ease.
The square root of 546 is 23.36664289109.
PROFESSOR PONY
She is correct!
TWILIGHT SPARKLE
I could ace a quiz on friendship's bliss,
but I wasn't prepared for this.
Will I fail or will I pass, I can't be sure.
SPIKE
She can't be sure.
TWILIGHT SPARKLE
My mind is sharp, my skills intact.
My heart is pure.
SPIKE
Her heart is pure.
TWILIGHT SPARKLE
Oh, I've taken my share of licks.
I've made it through the thin and thick.
But no, I wasn't...
SPIKE
Oh no, she wasn't...

TWILIGHT SPARKLE
Oh no, I wasn't...
SPIKE
Oh no, she wasn't...
TWILIGHT SPARKLE
No, I wasn't...
prepared for this!

Song: "The Ballad of the Crystal Ponies"
Episode: "The Crystal Empire, Part 1"
Lyrics by Meghan McCarthy
Music by Daniel Ingram

TWILIGHT SPARKLE
Princess Cadance needs our help.
Her magic will not last forever.
I think we can do it,
but we need to work together.
We have to get this right.
Yes, we have to make them see
we can save the Crystal ponies
with their history.

RAINBOW DASH
It says that they liked jousting.
RARITY
They flew a flag of many hues.
APPLEJACK
Made sweets of Crystal berries.
FLUTTERSHY
They had a petting zoo with tiny ewes.
PONIES
Oh, we have to get this right.
Yes, we have to make them see
we can save the Crystal ponies
with their history.
PINKIE PIE
There was a Crystal flügelhorn
that everypony liked to play.
TWILIGHT SPARKLE
And a Crystal Kingdom anthem.
Can you learn it in a day?
PONIES
Oh, we have to get this right.
Yes, we have to make them see
we can save the Crystal ponies
with their history.

Song: "The Success Song"
Episode: "The Crystal Empire, Part 2"
Lyrics by Meghan McCarthy
Music by Daniel Ingram

RARITY
You were prepared to do your best,
had what it takes to pass the test.
All those doubts you can dismiss.
Turns out you were prepared for this.
APPLEJACK
You clearly have just what it takes.
PINKIE PIE
To pass a test with such high stakes.
FLUTTERSHY
We knew for sure you would prevail.
RAINBOW DASH
Since when does Twilight Sparkle ever fail?
PONYVILLE PONIES
All those doubts that you can dismiss,
trust yourself and you cannot miss.
Turns out you were...
TWILIGHT SPARKLE
turns out I was...
PONYVILLE PONIES
turns out you were...
TWILIGHT SPARKLE
turns out I was...
RARITY
turns out you were...
PONYVILLE PONIES
prepared for this!

Song: "Babs Seed"
Episode: "One Bad Apple"
Lyrics by Cindy Morrow &
Daniel Ingram
Music by Daniel Ingram

APPLE BLOOM

First we thought that Babs
was so really, really sweet.
A new friend to have,
and it seemed like such a treat.

SCOOTALOO

But then we found the truth:
She's just a bully from the east.
She went from Babs,
yeah, to a bully and a beast!

APPLE BLOOM

Everywhere we turn,
she's just a step ahead!

CUTIE MARK CRUSADERS

Babs Seed! Babs Seed!
What we gonna do?
Got a bully on our tail,
gotta hide, we gotta bail.
Babs Seed! Babs Seed!
If she's after you,
you gotta run, we gotta flee,
gotta hurry, don't you see?
Babs Seed! Babs Seed!
She's just a bad, bad seed!

APPLE BLOOM

Hiding from a bully,
we know it isn't right,
but the Cutie Mark Crusaders,
we aren't lookin' for a fight!

SCOOTALOO

Oh, she'll go home soon
and then we'll have some peace again.

But for now we're stayin' out of her way
'til then.

APPLE BLOOM

Everywhere we turn,
she's just a step ahead.

CUTIE MARK CRUSADERS

Babs Seed! Babs Seed!
What we gonna do?
Gotta bully on our tail,
gotta hide, we gotta bail.
Babs Seed! Babs Seed!
If she's after you,
you gotta run, we gotta flee,
gotta hurry, don't you see?
Why so mean? Why so crude?
Why so angry? Why so rude?
Can't you be nice?
Can't we be friends?
Isn't it sad? Is this how it all ends?
Babs Seed, Babs Seed,
she's just a bad, bad...
Babs Seed, Babs Seed,
she's just a bad, bad...
Babs Seed, Babs Seed,
she's just a BAD, BAD SEED.

Song: "Raise This Barn"
Episode: "Apple Family Reunion"
Lyrics by Cindy Morrow
Music by Daniel Ingram

APPLEJACK

Raise this barn, raise this barn,
one, two, three, four.
Together we can raise this barn,
one, two, three, four.
Up, up, up go the beams.
Hammer those joints, work in teams.
Turn 'em round quick by the right elbow,
grab a new partner, here we go!
C'mon, Apple Family! Let's get to it!
Whooo-whee!
Raise this barn, raise this barn,
one, two, three, four.
Together we can raise this barn,
one, two, three, four.
Finish the frame, recycling wood,
workin' hard, you're doin' good!
Turn 'em round quick by the right elbow,
grab your partner, here we go!
Raise this barn, raise this barn,
one, two, three, four.
Together we can raise this barn,
one, two, three, four.
Slats of wood come off the ground.
Hold 'em up and nail them down.

Turn 'em round quick by the left elbow,
grab a new partner, here we go!
C'mon, Apples! Git 'er done!

APPLE BLOOM

Look at us, we're family.

APPLEJACK

Working together thankfully.

APPLE BLOOM

We Apples, we are proud to say...

APPLEJACK AND APPLE BLOOM

stick together the pony way.

APPLEJACK

Bow to your partner and circle right.
Get down if you're scared of heights!
Forward, back, and twirl around.
That barn's gonna be the best in town!
Yee-haw! Atta girl!

APPLE BLOOM

All right! Let's get to it!

APPLEJACK AND OTHERS

Raise this barn, raise this barn,
one, two, three, four.
Together we can raise this barn,
one, two, three, four.

APPLEJACK

Take your brushes, young and old.
Together paint it bright and bold.
Turn 'em round quick by the left elbow,
grab a new partner, here we go!

APPLEJACK AND OTHERS

We raised this barn, we raised this barn.
Yes, we did!
Together we sure raised this barn.
Yes, we did!
Being together counts the most.
We all came here from coast to coast.
All we need to strive to be
is part of the Apple FA-MI-LYYYY!

Song: "Morning in Ponyville"
Episode: "Magical Mystery Cure"
Lyrics by Mitch Larson
Music by Daniel Ingram

Song: "What My Cutie Mark Is Telling Me"
Episode: "Magical Mystery Cure"
Lyrics by Daniel Ingram
Music by Daniel Ingram

TWILIGHT SPARKLE

Morning in Ponyville shimmers,
morning in Ponyville shines,
and I know for absolute certain
that everything is certainly fine.
There's the mayor en route to her office.
There's the sofa clerk selling some quills.
Yes, my Ponyville is so gentle and still.
Can things ever go wrong?
I don't think they will.
Morning in Ponyville shimmers,
morning in Ponyville shines,
and I know for absolute certain
that everything is certainlyyyy—
RAINBOW DASH! That's not funny!

RARITY

Terribly sorry, darling. I'm afraid I'm not
good with the thundery ones.

TWILIGHT SPARKLE

[gasps] Something tells me everything
is not going to be fine.

RAINBOW DASH

These animals don't listen,
no, not one little bit.
They run around, out of control,
and throw their hissy fits.
It's up to me to stop them,
'cause plainly you can see,
it's got to be my destiny.
And it's what my cutie mark is telling me.

FLUTTERSHY

I try to keep them laughing,
put a smile upon their face.
But no matter what I try,
it seems a bit of a disgrace.
I have to entertain them;
it's there for all to see.
It's got to be my destiny.
And it's what my cutie mark is telling me.

A NEARBY PONY

[laughs]

> "We don't usually go into a story
> meeting knowing for sure that there will be a
> song in the episode. The decision to include one usually
> just comes from the process of fleshing out the episode. As
> we're figuring out the beats of the story, we start to see that an
> emotion a character is feeling might be better expressed through
> a song, or a montage we have planned calls for singing
> instead of just instrumental music behind it."
> —Meghan McCarthy, story editor

PINKIE PIE
I don't care much for pickin' fruit,
and plowin' fields ain't such a hoot.
No matter what I try I cannot fix
this busted water chute!
I've got so many chores to do;
it's no fun being me,
but it has to be my destiny.
'Cause that's what my cutie mark
is telling me.

APPLEJACK
Lookie here at what I made,
I think that it's a dress.
I know it doesn't look like much.
I'm under some distress.
Could y'all give me a hand here,
and help me fix this mess?
My destiny is not pretty,
but it's what my cutie mark is telling me.

RARITY
I'm in love with weather patterns,
but the others have concerns,

for I just gave them frostbite
over top of their sunburns.
I have to keep on trying,
for everyone can see....

RAINBOW DASH
it's got to be...

FLUTTERSHY
it's got to be...

PINKIE PIE
my destiny...

APPLEJACK
my destiny.

RARITY AND RAINBOW DASH
And it's what my cutie mark...

PINKIE PIE AND FLUTTERSHY
it's what my cutie mark...

ALL MAIN PONIES
yes, it's what my cutie mark is telling me.

Song: "I've Got to Find a Way"
Episode: "Magical Mystery Cure"
Lyrics by Daniel Ingram
Music by Daniel Ingram

TWILIGHT SPARKLE
I have to find a way
to make this all okay.
I can't believe this small mistake
could have caused so much heartache.
Oh why...?
Oh why...?
Losing promise, I don't know what to do.
Seeking answers, I fear I won't get
through to you....
Oh why...?
Oh why...?

"As we are
breaking a story
into acts and eventually
individual scenes, we start
to see where it might be nice
to have a song. The writer of the
episode knows at the outline stage
whether there will be a musical
number and writes the lyrics
into the script."
—Meghan McCarthy,
story editor

Song: "A True, True Friend"
Episode: "Magical Mystery Cure"
Lyrics by Daniel Ingram
Music by Daniel Ingram

TWILIGHT SPARKLE
A true, true friend helps a friend in need.
A friend will be there to help them see.
TWILIGHT SPARKLE AND FLUTTERSHY
A true, true friend helps a friend in need
to see the light that shines from a true,
true friend.
RAINBOW DASH
Um, hello?
Friend trapped inside, remember?
TWILIGHT SPARKLE
Rarity needs your help.
She's trying hard, doing what she can.
FLUTTERSHY
Would you try, just give it a chance?
You might find that you'll start to
understand.
TWILIGHT SPARKLE AND FLUTTERSHY
A true, true friend helps a friend in need.

A friend will be there to help you see.
A true, true friend helps a friend in need
to see the light that shines from a true,
true friend.
RAINBOW DASH
Uhhh, what just happened?
TWILIGHT SPARKLE
There's no time to explain...
but we need your help.
Applejack's trying to make dresses!
RAINBOW DASH
Say no more.
Applejack needs your help.
She's trying hard, doing what she can.
Would you try, just give it a chance?
You might find that you'll start to
understand....
**TWILIGHT SPARKLE, FLUTTERSHY,
AND RAINBOW DASH**
A true, true friend helps a friend in need.
A friend will be there to help them see.
A true, true friend helps a friend in need
to see the light that shines from a true,
true friend.

RARITY
Oh my!...What a terrible dream I had!
Or maybe I'm still having it.
TWILIGHT SPARKLE
Rarity, Pinkie Pie is about to lose the
Apple Farm.
We need Applejack's help....
RARITY
Lose the Apple Farm? Well, we can't let
that happen now, can we?
Pinkie Pie is in trouble.
We need to get there by her side.
We can try to do what we can now,
for together we can be her guide....
**TWILIGHT SPARKLE, FLUTTERSHY,
RAINBOW DASH, AND RARITY**
A true, true friend helps a friend in need.
A friend will be there to help them see.
A true, true friend helps a friend in need.
to see the light that shines from a true,
true frieeeend....
APPLEJACK
Yeee-haw! Now that's more like it!
What's next?
TWILIGHT SPARKLE
The townspeople are furious....
We need the old Pinkie Pie back!
APPLEJACK
I'm on it, I know just the thing.
The townspeople need you,
they've been sad for a while.
They march around, face a-frown,
and never seem to smile.
And if you feel like helpin',
we'd appreciate a lot
if you'd get up there and spread some
cheer from here to Canterlot....

PINKIE PIE
Come on, ponies! I wanna see you
SMILE!!!
TOWNSPONIES
PINKIE!!!
EVERYPONY
A true, true friend helps a friend in need.
A friend will be there to help them see.
A true, true friend helps a friend in need
to see the light...that shines...that shines!
From a true, true frieeeend!

Song: "Celestia's Ballad"
Episode: "Magical Mystery Cure"
Lyrics by Daniel Ingram
Music by Daniel Ingram

PRINCESS CELESTIA
You've come such a long, long way,
and I've watched you from that very
first day
to see how you might grow,
to see what you might do,
to see what you've been through,
and all the ways you've made me
proud of you.
It's time now for a new change to come.
You've grown up,
and your new life has begun.
To go where you will go,
to see what you will see,
to find what you will be,
for it's time for you
to fulfill your destinyyy....

Song: "Behold, Princess Twilight Sparkle"
Episode: "Magical Mystery Cure"
Lyrics by Daniel Ingram
Music by Daniel Ingram

EVERYPONY
The princess Twilight cometh!
Behold! Behold!
The princess here before us!
Behold! Behold!
Behold! Behold!
The princess Twilight cometh!
Behold! Behold!
The princess is,
the princess is here!

Song: "Life in Equestria"
Episode: "Magical Mystery Cure"
Lyrics by Mitch Larson
Music by Daniel Ingram

TWILIGHT SPARKLE
Life in Equestria shimmers,
life in Equestria shines,
and I know for absolute certain...
PONIES
that everything, yes, everything,
yes, that everything, yes, that everything
is certainly fine.
Is fiiineee!

"There are actually quite a few songs I've found myself singing when no one's around, but the one that stands out for me the most is 'Celestia's Ballad.' As animation supervisor over the past three seasons, I actually got a little choked up the first time I watched the finished sequence where Princess Celestia shows Twilight flashbacks from her life. It was almost like seeing flashbacks from the past three years of my life!"
—Ishi Ruddell, animation director

"It amazes me to think of
how deeply children and fans of all
ages are embracing the DNA and true
essence of the My Little Pony brand. We
are thrilled the brand has transcended age and
gender globally because of our socially relevant
messages of friendship, tolerance, and that it is okay
to be who you uniquely are. It is quite wonderful
and has been an honor to be part of this new
generation of My Little Pony, and of all that
the brand represents."
—Donna Tobin, senior director
of global brand strategy and
marketing, Hasbro

FRIENDSHIP FANATICS

BOOOM

My Little Pony Is Taking Over!

Trends will always come and go, but none have taken the world by storm like the *Friendship is Magic* movement. Kids, parents, and fans of all ages have been mesmerized by this undeniable phenomenon. But what is it about these lovable ponies that have people celebrating the world over? Sure, they're charming, sweet, and all-around awesome, but there's more to these little ponies than meets the eye. In a market flooded with animated programs and requisite toy lines, My Little Pony has excelled because of its combination of branding and substance. The equation is simple: fun, bright characters + engaging storytelling mixed with a positive message = a perfect blend of entertainment and education that's fun for families of all shapes and sizes. Kids love the characters, parents like the messages, and fans love everything in between.

The *My Little Pony* animated series is filled with magic, wonder, and escapism just as any good children's program should be. In a saturated television landscape, it can be difficult to project a positive message without coming across as heavy-handed. But the dazzling ponies of Equestria and their quest to become the best ponies

PONY
FRIENDS
FOREVER

P.F.F.

they can be have proven it's possible to make entertaining, quality television that teaches a thing or two in the process. Whether it's Applejack's Southern charm, Rainbow

Dash's boundless energy, or Twilight Sparkle's lovable neurosis, each pony is known for her distinct and unique personality. Viewers see themselves reflected in each character's individuality and learn that it's important to be who you are. They celebrate their favorite character's triumphs and learn along with them when they make a mistake. The diverse cast is filled with relatable representations of a variety of distinct personality types. Conveying these positive lessons are frenetic and exciting stories that use music, dance, and a crisp pace to keep young people involved and energized. Episodes are simple to understand, are smartly written, and feature subtle adult humor to keep parents watching alongside their kids.

Bright personalities, bold colors, and high energy have been proven to capture attention, but *My Little Pony* also empowers young girls to be anything they want to be in life. As simple as that tenet may sound, it can be difficult to find programming with a strong feminine point of view that doesn't shy away from

"It does surprise me that fans have connected so strongly with the Elements of Harmony. And the fandom has really impressed me with where they've taken the philosophy of the Elements. They have done lots of charity work and fund-raisers, feeling that philanthropy is part of the message of the Elements."
—Amy Keating Rogers, writer

confronting the choices a young girl may be faced with. While some girls enjoy dressing up, others like to play sports. While some *ponies* love brushing their mane, others enjoy a hard day's work. *My Little Pony* encourages girls to be girly in their own special way, but only if they *want* to be. In

"I'm not at all surprised at the fans' love of the show. It's fun, funny, and full of adventure, but never shies away from the sincerity of emotion and heart inherent in the characters. I really believe the fans identify and admire those qualities in our main ponies. They represent the qualities we should all aspire to have when choosing our own friends: honesty, loyalty, generosity, kindness, and laughter."
—Jim Miller, storyboard supervisor

Ponyville, there's room for everypony to be who they want to be and embrace their talents and individuality. The characters refuse to be easily defined and often encourage one another to try new things so that they have a chance to grow and learn.

The word *family* means different things to different people, but we can all agree that a family loves and supports one another unconditionally. That's why parents connect so deeply to the bonds among Twilight Sparkle, Pinkie Pie, and the rest of the

"My favorite fan art is a 'Chomper' drawing done by my daughter when she came in to hang out with me at work one day. It's a burger-eating shark-pony drawing that she did for a coworker who loves sharks. She wanted to help the director out with ideas for new pony designs. The director [James Wootton] took the drawing to the art director, Ridd Sorensen, to slick it up a bit and then handed it back to my girl for final approval. She and I were very touched with this gesture."
—Sherann Johnson, storyboard artist

"I am definitely honored to be a significant part of such an amazing show and cultural phenomenon. As a parent myself, I'm glad that other parents feel that the work we do and the stories we tell are something they feel comfortable sharing with their children, as I do."
—Jayson Thiessen, supervising director

ponies in Equestria. In addition to its entertainment value, *My Little Pony* serves as a teaching tool for families to use at home when illustrating important life lessons. As Twilight Sparkle learns the importance of sharing and friendship, parents can use her experiences to educate their children and pass along these valuable messages. Musical numbers like the "Sharing/Caring Song" are designed to engage kids by making the message fun, energetic, and relatable.

Nostalgia often plays a part in popular culture, and many parents have welcomed *My Little Pony* into their homes because they grew up with it. Moms share their childhood love of the brand, which helps them relate to the

"I was on vacation in Austin, Texas, during a record-breaking heat wave, and while walking along the sidewalk near my hotel in South Congress, I saw in the distance what looked to be a person in a large pink mascot costume. Initially, I dismissed it as someone on their way to a sporting event of some kind and continued chatting with my friends, but as we passed the pink mascot, I noticed a balloon cutie mark on the hip of the costume. This was Pinkie Pie! Someone was dressed head to toe in this fuzzy costume in 110-degree heat! Now that's dedication!"
—Devon Cody, producer

"As a parent, I've had to sit through my share of shows with my kids so I understand how great it is to find ones that we enjoy watching together, and that have a positive impact on them. I had a mom come up to me and tell me that when her sons start to argue, she just has to say, 'What would Pinkie Pie do?' and instead of continuing to fight, they try to calmly resolve their differences. One of the many joys of working on this show is knowing that I'm not just getting to write funny stories, but that I'm putting something with a really positive message out into the world."
—Meghan McCarthy, story editor

kids in the process. Instead of stagnating, *My Little Pony* has evolved to include modern attitudes toward family, community, and acceptance. The characters and their continued evolution serve to reignite a fondness felt by parents, which they, in turn, pass along to the next generation.

It can be argued that younger generations have become desensitized to violence because of the deluge of images shown to them on television and the Internet, and in the news media. Though *My Little Pony* rests comfortably in the realm of fantasy, parents can rest assured that even the most perilous situations that the characters may find themselves in can always be solved

"One day I received a package hand-delivered by some fans from out of town. It was an incredible My Little Pony poster that they had custom-designed and signed by all the prominent musicians in the fan community at the time. It's a beautiful piece of work and a very touching gesture from the community. I had it framed, and it hangs in my studio today."
—Daniel Ingram, song composer

by a nonviolent resolution. The solutions are always clear, clever, and positive.

My Little Pony may be aimed squarely at younger audiences, but the universal appeal of the series for all ages is recognized by the show's creator, Lauren Faust, as one of the secrets to its success. But what keeps teen and adult fans engaged in a show meant for kids? The message of *Friendship is Magic* is a universal one, and fans of all ages connect deeply to the show's sense of camaraderie and fellowship.

"It's a good feeling knowing that kids are not only enjoying the show for its entertainment value, but that they are getting something deeper out of it as well."
—Ridd Sorensen, art director

"A fan I spoke to told me that Cindy Morrow's episode 'Griffon the Brush Off' really had a strong effect on him. This fan always felt that he needed to please everyone in order to have friends. He would even change his personality to do this. But in watching this episode, he learned that he just needed to be himself like Pinkie was. If someone liked him, great! If not, then they weren't his friend to begin with."
—Amy Keating Rogers, writer